APOLLOS OF THE N(

APOLLOS OF THE NORTH

SELECTED POEMS OF GEORGE BUCHANAN AND ARTHUR JOHNSTON

WITH ENGLISH VERSIONS
AND AN INTRODUCTION BY

Robert Crawford

FOREWORD BY

Edwin Morgan

For Alan and Susan Milligan
fortunati ambo

This edition published in Great Britain in 2006
by Polygon, an imprint of Birlinn Ltd
West Newington House
10 Newington Road
Edinburgh EH9 1QS

www.birlinn.co.uk

ISBN 10: 1 904598 81 1
ISBN 13: 978 1 904598 81 7

Introduction and translations copyright © Robert Crawford 2006
Foreword copyright © Edwin Morgan, 2006

All rights reserved. No part of this publication may be reproduced,
stored, or transmitted in any form, or by any means, electronic, mechanical
or photocopying, without the express written permission of the publisher.

The publishers acknowledge subsidy from

towards the publication of this volume

Robert Crawford thanks the University of St Andrews and
the Arts and Humanities Research Council for a semester's research
leave during which he was able to work on this book.

British Library Cataloguing-in-Publication Data
A catalogue record of this book is available from the British Library

Typeset in Golden Cockerel by Koinonia, Bury, Lancashire
and printed and bound in Great Britain by
Thomson Litho, East Kilbride

Contents

Foreword ix
Acknowledgements x
Introduction xiii

GEORGE BUCHANAN
from *Franciscanus* 2
The Exorcist 3

Andreae Goveano 6
Inscription for the Tomb of the Portuguese Humanist André de Gouvea 7

Ad Rectorem Scholae Conimbricae Mursam, etc. 8
Beleago 9

Ad Eundem Invictissimum Regem De Hoc Commentario Georgius Buchananus 12
A Commendation of the *Commentarius* of Diogio de Teive to King João III of Portugal 13

In Polyonymum 14
To the Opposite of Anon 15

Brasilia 16
Brazil 17

In Zoilum 16
Against Zoilus 17

Ad Peiridem Lenam 18
To a Bawd called Peiris 19

Ad Eandem [Leonoram] 20
Mair Leonora 21

E Graeco Simonidis 20
From the Greek of Simonides 21

Desiderium Lutetiae 22
Longing for Paris 23

XXIII 28
The Twenty-third Psalm Paraphrased during Imprisonment at the Hands of the Inquisition in Portugal 29

Adventus in Galliam 30
Coming to France 31

De Equo Elogium 32
Horse Hymn 33

Jacobo Sylvio 32
On James Wood 33

De Nicotiana Falso Nomine Medicaea Appellata 34
Can Damage Your Health 35

Jacobo IV. Regi Scotorum 36
To James IV, King of Scots 37

Maria Regina Scotiae Puella 36
The Young Girl Mary, Queen of Scots 37

Francisci Valesi et Mariae Stuartae, Regum Franciae et Scotiae, Epithalamium 38
Epithalamium for Francis of Valois and Mary Stuart, Monarchs of France and Scotland 39

Ad Mariam Illustrissimam Scotorum Reginam 54
To the Noblest Mary, Queen of Scots, with a Book of Psalms 55

Magdalanae Valesiae Reginae Scotorum, XVI Aetatis Anno Exstinctae 56
Madeleine of Valois, Queen of Scots, Dead at Sixteen 57

Mutuus Amor 56
The Bond of Love 57

D. Gualtero Haddono Magistro Libellorum Supplicum Serenissimae Angliae Reginae 58
To Lord Walter Haddon, Petition Master of the Most Serene Queen of England 59

Rogero Aschamo Anglo 62
For Roger Ascham, Englishman 63

E Graeco Simonidis 62
From the Greek of Simonides 63

Ad Henricum Scotorum Regem 62
To Henry Darnley, King of Scots 63

In Syllam 64
Against Sulla 65

Laurentius Valla 64
Lorenzo Valla, Humanist 65

from *De Sphaera* 66
On the Planet 67

Ioannis Calvini Epicedium 70
Elegy for John Calvin 71

Ad Theodorum Bezam 74
To Theodore Beza 75

Hymnus Matutinus ad Christum 76
Morning Hymn to Christ 77

In Iulium II Pontificem 78
Oan Paip J 2 79

In Eandem Romam 78
The Pope of Rome Again 79
Ite, Missa Est 78
Go, Mass is Over 79
Imago ad Peregre Venientes Religionis Ergo 80
The Image to the Pilgrims 81

ARTHUR JOHNSTON

from *Musarum Elogia* 84
Four Muses' Sentences 85

Edinburgum 86
Edinburgh 87

Glasgua 88
Glasgow 89

Sterlinum 90
Stirling 91

Andreapolis 92
St Andrews 93

Taodunum 94
Dundee 95

Mons Rosarum 96
Montrose 97

Brechinum 98
Brechin 99

De Aberdonia Urbe 100
On the City of Aberdeen 101

Elginum 102
Elgin 103

from *Nobiles Scoti* and from *Episcopi Scoti* 104
Scots Lords, Scots Bishops 105

De Anatomica Sectione, a Iulio Casserio Placentino Patavii Exhibita 106
On an Anatomical Dissection Exhibited at Padua by Julius Casserius
    of Placentia 107

De Reginae Choreis 106
On the Queen's Dances 107

De Comite Hollandio 108
On the Earl of Holland 109

Insignia Equestria Divi Georgii 110
Insignia of the Knights of Saint George 111

De Columbario Eudoxi Praesulis 110
Bishop Eudoxus' Doocot 111
De Balagaunio Eiusdem Equo 112
Balagaunius 113
Ad Illustrem Comitem Gordonium, Marchionis Huntlaei Filium, Natu Maximum 112
To the Illustrious Earl Gordon, Eldest Son of the Marquis of Huntly 113
De Eiusdem Lapsu ex Equo 114
On the Fall of the Earl Gordon from his Horse 115
De Gulielmo Gordonio Rothimaeo, et Georgio Gordonio Caesis 116
On William Gordon of Rothiemay and George Gordon, Killed in Action 117
De Iohanne Gordonio, Vicecomite de Melgein, et Iohanne Gordonio de Rothimay in Arce Frendriaca Combustis 118
The Atrocity at Frendrocht 119
from *Ad Robertum Baronium* 126
To Robert Baron 127
In Obitum M. Davidis Balantini de Kinnochar, Ecclesiastae 130
On the Death of the Reverend David Ballantyne of Kilconquhar 131
Ad Iamisonum Pictorem, de Anna Cambella, Heroina 132
To Jamesone the Artist, About the Splendid Lady Anne Campbell 133
Tumulus Nobilissimae Heroinae, Annae Cambellae, Marchionissae de Huntley 134
The Tomb of the Noblest Heroine Anne Campbell, Marchioness of Huntly 135
In Obitum Gulielmi Forbesii Cragivarrii 136
Obituary for William Forbes of Craigievar 137
In Obitum Iohannae Ionstonae 138
On the Death of Joanna Johnston 139
De Horto Suo 142
My Book Garden 143
De Gulielmo Drummondo 142
On William Drummond 143
Saltatrix 144
The Dancing Art 145
De Hylo Concionatore 144
On the Popular Haranguer 'Hylus' Wood 145
Inneruria 146
Inverurie 147
De Loco Suo Natali 148
Birthplace 149

Index of Poem Titles 150

Foreword

Latin was one of Scotland's literary languages for many centuries, and the reawakening of its neglected or forgotten European spirit is the task Robert Crawford gives himself in this remarkable, thought-provoking book. 'Task' is perhaps the wrong term to employ of a work which has been compiled with so much gusto, taking many risks and offering the modern reader so many surprises. In the sixteenth and seventeenth centuries George Buchanan and Arthur Johnston were regarded as notable Scottish poets, even though they wrote in Latin. Through this bilingual anthology, with its polemical but informative introduction, Crawford both deplores the disappearance of Latin from so many educational facilities and makes his case for the vigour of poetry in a 'dead' language – dead, but will not lie down decently and die.

The translations range from close to free, and are not afraid to use anachronisms. They offer an extraordinary variety of subject-matter, from formal celebration of a royal wedding to outspokenly satirical character-assassinations, from a public anatomical dissection to the feats of a multi-sexual prostitute, from praise of horses to scurrilities on popes. Johnston, a gentler soul than Buchanan, provides delightfully witty eulogies of Scottish towns, including Edinburgh and Glasgow, Elgin and Dundee, and has attractive thumbnail sketches of William Drummond the poet and George Jamesone the artist. Buchanan, the Juvenal of Killearn, has a scarifying piece of verbal fireworks attacking Beleago, a Portuguese colleague at Coimbra whom he suspected of shopping him to the Inquisition, and a strange elegy on Calvin which turns a searchlight on the reformer and gives it an unexpected twist.

It is a pleasure to recommend this sprightly book, by means of which one further element of the great jigsaw of Scotland falls into place.

Edwin Morgan

Acknowledgements

In putting together this book I have been helped by poets and scholars over several centuries. I would like to pay tribute to Thomas Ruddiman (1674–1757), the great Scottish Latinist, whose edition of George Buchanan's *Opera omnia* (1715) provides the base text for Buchanan's Latin poems. From the nineteenth century, Sir William Duguid Geddes's first two volumes of *Musa Latina Aberdonensis* (Aberdeen: New Spalding Club, 1892 and 1895) contain many poems and much scholarly and biographical information about Arthur Johnston. Geddes's splendid edition supplied not only the Latin texts of the Johnston poems I selected but also most of my biographical information. Geddes's inclusion of English prose 'arguments' of the poems was invaluable to someone whose Latin stopped at secondary school level and has eroded ever since. In the twentieth century the texts selected and the translations made by Paul J. McGinnis and Arthur H. Williamson for their book, *George Buchanan, The Political Poetry* (Edinburgh: Scottish History Society, 1995) were essential to the making of *Apollos of the North*.

I first met George Buchanan in Church Street, St Andrews, where, in the much lamented John Hooker Books, I bought *George Buchanan, Prince of Poets* by Philip J. Ford and W. S. Watt (Aberdeen: Aberdeen University Press, 1982). Its prose translations of Buchanan's *Miscellaneorum Liber* were wonderfully helpful. So was I. D. McFarlane's great biographical-scholarly study *Buchanan* (London: Duckworth, 1981) which supplied lots of the biographical information about Buchanan in my introduction and helped me get a clearer sense of that poet's milieu – not to mention alerting me to some of the treasures in the Special Collections Department of the Library of the University of St Andrews. For their help I would like to thank Dr Alice Crawford, Mrs Rachel Hart, Mrs Elizabeth Henderson, Ms Moira Mackenzie, and Dr Norman Reid of that Department. Like McFarlane and George Buchanan before him, I work at St Andrews, and there I first met Roger Green, now Professor of Humanity at the University of Glasgow. I am hugely in his debt for encouragement, and particularly for sending me his article 'Davidic psalm and Horatian ode: five poems of George Buchanan' (*Renaissance Studies*, XIV.1, 2000), without which I could not have worked on Buchanan's paraphrase of Psalm XXIII. Professor Green's unpublished prose translation also made it possible for me to make a verse version of the Johnston poem which appears here as 'The Atrocity at Frendrocht'. Unlike me, Roger Green is a professional scholar of Scottish Latin poetry, and I hope that his plans for a full edition of the *Delitiae* bear fruit. I hope also that we shall see one day a full, parallel text edition of the works of Buchanan.

Invitations to speak and read at the School of Classics at St Andrews, the West of Scotland Classical Association and the universities of Oxford and Yale helped me re-establish contact with fragments of my own schoolboy Classics. The work and occasional remarks of my St Andrews Scottish Studies Centre colleague Professor Roger Mason have been extremely useful. Mrs Frances Mullan, secretary of SASSC, worked wonders as she helped format the typescript. The *Oxford Dictionary of National Biography* entries for Buchanan (by D. M. Abbott) and Johnston (by my former St Andrews colleague Dr Nicola Royan) helped keep me somewhat on the rails. Most helpful and most fun was the sustaining company of my colleagues John Burnside, Douglas Dunn, Lorna Hutson, Kathleen Jamie, Andrew Murphy, Don Paterson and Neil Rhodes. It is good to be with poets as well as scholars! The friendship of Henry Hart, W. N. Herbert and David Kinloch over the years has taught me much too about what it means to have a sustaining international group of poet friends, but the most intimate sustenance has come from the love of my wife, Alice, and our children, Blyth and Lewis. They have found my obsession with long-dead Latin poets decidedly bothersome at times, and I appreciate their patience. Any mistakes in what follows are entirely my own – and sometimes deliberate.

This book was completed while on research leave granted by the University of St Andrews and the Arts and Humanities Research Council. I am grateful to both. The English versions of Arthur Johnston's 'Glasgow', 'St Andrews', 'To Robert Baron' and 'Birthplace' are reprinted from Robert Crawford, *Selected Poems* (Cape, 2005) with kind permission of Random House. At Polygon, Hugh Andrew, Neville Moir, Alison Rae and Sarah Ream have been a pleasure to work with. Thanks for Polygon's readiness in the third millennium to become a major publisher of Scottish Latin.

Introduction

Latin is one of the great languages of Scottish literature. For a thousand years it was Scotland's most important written medium, and until at least the eighteenth century it remained a vital cultural channel, an engine of the Scottish Enlightenment. In comparison, English (which displaced Latin as Scotland's main medium of international communication) is a relative newcomer. Gaelic, spoken across most of Scotland for part of the early Middle Ages, linked speakers in Scotland with communities in Ireland; later, Scots language connected Scottish people with some communities in England. But the international language of long-distance communication, the language of art, knowledge and international diplomacy that linked Scotland to Europe and beyond, was Latin. Latin is the language of the 'Altus Prosator' attributed to St Columba – the first great poem connected with the territory we now call Scotland. A thousand years later, Latin is still the language of the Renaissance poets in this book. Using this tongue, they felt connected not only to other Scottish Latin poets (of whom they were proud), but also to a sophisticated multicultural audience across the Western world; like that audience, these poets drew on the poetic resources of a language that linked them directly to such ancient poets as Virgil, Ovid and Horace. Latin was the voice of Europe, a language Scottish poets loved.

Recently, however, none of Scotland's minority languages has fared worse than Latin. For a century it has been under relentless and often state-supported attack. This has deprived Scots of a full sense not just of their own multicultural and many-tongued past, but has also helped sap the kind of confident internationalism which made Scots like George Buchanan and Arthur Johnston at once so cosmopolitan and so confidently, sometimes quirkily Scottish. Across Scotland, a great tradition of the teaching of Classics – Latin and Greek – has been smashed. As the twentieth century developed, Latin and Greek teaching in schools atrophied, and even in the universities it was savagely cut back. A combination of prejudice, naivety, parochialism and Thatcherite economics may have been to blame, but this process hardly resounds to Scotland's glory.

Latin may have been associated by many with the Catholic Church, whose liturgical tradition continued to value such things as the Latin Mass; in a twentieth century where anti-Irish-Catholic and more general anti-Catholic Protestant prejudice were strong (especially in the West), this did not help those who sought to champion Latin; a Protestant-derived (and now sometimes anti-English) strain in Scottish culture always tends to defend vernacular language over formal speech. This reinforces a suspicion of Latin, though even Robert Burns, our greatest vernacular writer, learned much from his favourite Scottish poet, the Classically-educated Robert Fergusson. In fact during the Renaissance, Latin, the language of the Roman empire, then of the Roman Church throughout the Middle Ages, was far from an exclusively orthodox Catholic language; in Scotland it had been used vigorously and even viciously by Protestant Reformers like George Buchanan, but you need some access to Latin education to appreciate that. In reaction against Protestant prejudice, a number of distinguished twentieth-century Scottish cultural figures including Edwin Muir and Hugh MacDiarmid presented the Protestant Reformation as something that killed off art and poetry. This reaction is equally naive (as again the spiky poetic example of George Buchanan demonstrates), but it helped to enshrine distorted views of Scotland's cultural past which still persist, and which have contributed further to the devaluing of Latin in Scotland.

Latin was seen by others as elitist. Again, the roots of this view may be traced to the Protestant Reformation, with its campaigns to allow people direct access to the Bible in their own vernacular language, rather than having to approach it via a Roman Catholic priestly elite who knew the Latin of the Vulgate Bible. Centuries later, it was easy for such arguments to turn into straightforward anti-Catholic and anti-Latin prejudice in a predominantly Protestant twentieth-century Scotland. More than that, after many years when the British Empire was mapped on to the ancient empire of Classical Rome, and when so many Scots fought for and managed the British Empire, training in Latin and Greek was often a passport into the elite corps of the Oxbridge-led British Civil Service – a way to become a mandarin. A reaction against empire and its elite, mandarin ruling castes brought a reaction against the teaching of Classics. Besides, as late-twentieth-century Thatcherism most brutally implied, Latin and Greek were useless: they were not immediately economically productive. The Classical and older Scottish emphasis on what the Greeks had called the 'polis' and the Scottish Enlightenment had termed 'civil society' held little appeal for an ideology that maintained (as Margaret Thatcher did in her Edinburgh 'Sermon on the Mound') that there was no such thing as society. Since they manifestly did not make money, and championed values of a culture that treasured more than just cash, the school and university subjects of Latin and Greek were, even more than other 'useless' Arts subjects, potential sites of intellectual and artistic resistance to a Thatcherite vision. They had to be swept aside. It was during the Thatcher era that the Classics Department of Aberdeen University was axed. Aberdeen, a beacon of Latin Humanist scholarship in Scotland in the Renaissance, the university of Arthur Johnston and the 'Musa Latina Aberdonensis' so lovingly celebrated by its late-nineteenth-century University Principal, turned its back on the language and culture of some of its greatest intellectual distinctions. Other school and university Classics departments went to the wall across Britain; in Scotland children were steered away from Latin (too difficult, 'useless', 'dead') and university departments shrank.

Looking back on this shameful period, it is evident that the most effective defence against the attack on Latin and Greek within Scottish culture was carried on principally by creative artists, especially perhaps poets. As in Ireland where, in the period surrounding the tragic closing of the Classics Department at Queen's University, Belfast, poets such as Seamus Heaney and Michael Longley in works like *Seeing Things, The Cure at Troy* and 'Ceasefire' drew repeatedly and committedly on Latin and Greek works in their art, so in Scotland even as the state and local education authorities eroded the teaching of Classics, artists turned repeatedly to Classical learning and subject matter. Though there is no extended study of the influence of Latin and Greek on modern Scottish writers, it is obvious that the impact was both deep and wide-ranging, extending across English, Scots and Gaelic. Where Edwin Muir had written of Troy and Hugh MacDiarmid had made versions of Greek and Latin poets (including, on one occasion, Arthur Johnston), later generations of Scottish poets treasured and deployed a sense of their Classical inheritance in their work. The Scots-language poet Douglas Young studied Classics at St Andrews, then at New College, Oxford; the Gaelic poet George Campbell Hay studied Classics at Corpus Christi College, Oxford. In the 2005 Polygon collected edition of his poetry, there is a passage where, in interview, the English-language poet Norman MacCaig, who had studied Latin and Greek at Edinburgh University, realised late in life how much that experience had meant to his work:

> Classical writing is generally very formal. I don't mean in the sense of formal manners, but very interested in shape more than colour, slightly more than colour. It keeps to the fact, which Romanticism doesn't. Romanticism glorifies and splatters the object with the

writer's feelings, which I hate. Celtic art is very classical. In old Celtic art, all of their arts, songs, poems, sculpture ... are very formal and I think I have always loved form, unconsciously. This is hindsight. But probably that's the reason I chose to take Classics at the university. And my native preference was, of course, reinforced by the study of Classics. So if I write a poem about an emotion, I don't inflate it. I write and I write as honestly as I can.

When the Classically-educated Gaelic poet Sorley MacLean wishes to praise a boat he calls it 'a Ghreugaich choimhlionta' (perfect Greek) in his poem 'Am Bàta Dubh' (The Black Boat) which juxtaposes Ithaca and Uist; like his friends the Classicist Douglas Young (who translated Aristophanes into Scots) and Robert Garioch (who translated one poem and two plays by George Buchanan into Scots), MacLean was schooled in Latin at a time when Latin and Greek were much more readily available in the Scottish educational curriculum. In his books *The Democratic Intellect* and *The Crisis of the Democratic Intellect*, George Davie showed how such an availability was championed through the tradition or potent myth of the 'democratic intellect' upheld in the early twentieth century by figures like the St Andrews University Classicist John Burnet, whose work was admired by poets as different as Hugh MacDiarmid and T. S. Eliot. At St Andrews, Burnet's successors such as Douglas Young and William Lorimer maintained a strong living link between Classical scholarship and creative writing, especially between Classics and Scots vernacular literature. Even in the last three decades when what we might call in shorthand the crass mentality of 'Thatcherite economics' (the aggressive opposite of 'art for art's sake') has done most damage to Scotland's sense of her Classical inheritance, Scottish writers have consistently reminded their readers of its value.

Alasdair Gray's *Lanark* (1981), often seen as the watershed of recent Scottish fiction, begins by plunging *in medias res* (into the midst of things) like Virgil's *Aeneid* and other Classical epics, and Gray draws on both the *Aeneid* and on Classical scholarship in the book. Shortly after *Lanark*, there appeared in 1984 William Lorimer's translation of the New Testament from Greek into Scots. This work by a retired St Andrews University Classics Professor became an international success, and can be recognised as the greatest work of Scots prose – as well as a remarkable product of the Classical tradition in Scotland. More recently, works from Liz Lochhead's *Medea* to Don Paterson's wink at Plutarch, Romulus and Remus in 'Letter to the Twins' from his collection *Landing Light* (2003) and W. N. Herbert's 2002 *Big Bumper Book of Troy* assert the validity of the Classics to contemporary

Scottish culture. In the long process of assembling an anthology of *Scottish Religious Poetry* (2000) James McGonigal and I persuaded Edwin Morgan to translate both Columba's 'Altus Prosator' and George Buchanan's elegy for Calvin; this led to Morgan's further translation of a Latin poem about Bannockburn. Contemporary Scottish writers as different as A. L. Kennedy and Alan Massie are ready to pay tribute to the importance of Latin and Greek literature, though surely the most arresting Scottish work with Classical material has been produced by Ian Hamilton Finlay who has brought Daphne, Apollo and the disturbing power of the Latin and Greek inheritance into a dazzling confrontation with contemporary assumptions about state power, revolution and freedom in the militant pastoral of his garden at Little Sparta, some miles south-west from the Calton Hill acropolis of a sometimes startled Athens of the North.

Though a crude and naive ideology of 'relevance' may choose not to notice the full Classical significance of Calton Hill or Little Sparta, may fail to consider how the 'neoclassical' Enlightenment Edinburgh New Town relates to Scottish and European traditions of the Classics, and may dismiss as 'elitist' anything to do with Classics, we should be careful that we are not simply enslaved to the prejudices of the past. Even if the tide of Thatcherism has ebbed from Scotland, leaving behind it the 'settled will of the Scottish people' that led to the great gift of achieved Devolution, there is yet the danger of a 'soft Thatcherite' mentality which values the arts and scholarship only in terms of their power to generate short-term profit as 'cultural industries' or their immediate social utility. This is a bureaucrat's view of the arts, one which may be bound up with the tedious managerial prose of Cultural Commissions, but too often fails to connect with the imaginations of poets, artists, composers, or with any other imaginations. There are no votes in Latin. So politicians will regard any mention of it as quixotic. Yet Latin and the wider Classical tradition have been essential to the imagination in Scotland for at least fifteen centuries: from St Columba to Ian Hamilton Finlay, from Gavin Douglas to Liz Lochhead and James MacMillan. In the early twenty-first century some of the most challenging and beautiful recent artistic work internationally reveals a deep engagement with Classical language, literature and culture: whether in North America through the work of Anne Carson, in Ireland through the poetry of Seamus Heaney and Michael Longley, in England through the work of Tony Harrison and Geoffrey Hill, or on continental Europe from Michel Deguy's 'Passim' to Arvo Pärt's 'Te Deum' and 'Berliner Messe'. Today it would be as parochial as it would have been in the Renaissance to turn our backs on the imaginative challenges and possibilities of the Classics.

Indeed, Scotland's Latin tradition, blending internationalism with native confidence, playfully and sometimes painfully engaging with past and present, does have a disturbing relevance for twenty-first-century Scots, uncertain whether their country is a remote postcolonial zone or a hotspot economy of knowledge. Reading a Latin poet such as George Buchanan can be uneasy, because we have to confront questions of oppression, sectarianism and racism in our own culture; such unease, though, is just what Scotland needs if it is to have a full and nuanced sense of itself, an awareness of what it has done and of what it is capable of doing. To include in our sense of Scotland an awareness of the literary culture produced in one of our greatest minority languages – Latin – is not to escape into some scholarly Shangri-La, but to face up to the fact that often we would like to cosmeticise, oversimplify and phonily market the culture that has helped to make the Scotland we now inhabit. It was a culture of ambition, violence, beauty, internationalism, ideological quarrels and very local pride. If all that sounds familiar, it is because, whatever our colour, faith, sex or gender, as contemporary Scots it is our inheritance. We may not agree with them, we may smile at them, but George Buchanan and Arthur Johnston should not be forgotten or airbrushed away, any more than should Irvine Welsh or Mary, Queen of Scots. They are essential to the complex grain of a culture which, like any other, is inflected by its pasts as well as by a multiplicity of elements in its present. To live as if any part of that past or that present does not exist is to live a lie. A Scotland without Latin might seem (though only to unimaginative people) economically convenient. But it is still a lie.

Sadly, class warfare in Scotland has tended to deprive working-class people and many middle-class people of access to Classical languages. Today in many parts of the country only if you are well enough off and if you have no scruples about paying for private education can you get schooling in Latin and Greek for your children. In the earlier parts of the twentieth century Latin was a language taught to bright kids. Streaming in schools tended to mean that the children who seemed cleverest at school were encouraged to learn Latin and Greek. For some this meant that Classics had kudos; for others it was associated with snobbery. Both these attitudes are apparent in Muriel Spark's *The Prime of Miss Jean Brodie*. Reading Classical writers encouraged students to think deeply about such issues as democracy, slavery, how society should be run, empire and other matters which, perhaps, some twentieth-century politicians wanted to keep as the intellectual preserve of only a few people in an age when mass socialism and independence movements around the globe threatened the *status quo*. Artists fought, though, to free the latent power of the Classics.

It is no accident that the radical Lewis Grassic Gibbon, author of a book recently touted as Scotland's favourite novel – *Sunset Song* (1932) – was also the author of *Spartacus* (1933), a revolutionary fiction about a Roman slave uprising which draws on the Classical historians Plutarch and Sallust. Later, though, the very fact that Classical education had been the preserve of only an elite seemed a good reason to get rid of it, in the interests of comprehensive democracy. For a time, too, it was thought that removal of Classical languages from the school curriculum would encourage the growth of Modern Languages. Instead, though, as ancient language provision was reduced, the teaching of modern languages also contracted.

Schoolteachers were discouraged from teaching children difficult matters of style or content like verbal nuance, syntax or how different languages showed the world in different ways. Out went Classics which gave depth to hard questions such as those about the relationship between imperial freedom and security. Instead, more useful 'vocational' teaching emphasised practical skills that would be useful for obedient workers in a successful high-capitalist economy. In a nutshell, rather than reading the poetry of Sappho or Ovid, it made better educational sense to equip someone to work in a call centre. If your parents were rich enough, though, you would probably not have to work in a call centre and so your parents could afford to buy you an education in Latin and Greek. If you come from a socially disadvantaged background, you might just be allowed to watch *Troy* or *Gladiator*, but you'll have no business getting access to the languages of the poetry of Homer or Virgil.

This is a very socially conservative kind of education, which aims to limit the imaginative as well as the economic horizons of most people. Apparently anti-elitist, it perpetuates an elite who have ready access to the kinds of imaginative and sophisticated artistic riches represented by poetry in Latin and Greek, while the rest of society has to make do with tabloid television. Such a society mixes up having access to literacy with having access to magnificent literature. It champions access to the arts, but doesn't worry about the quality of the arts to which most people have access. In such a society there is still a place for detailed knowledge of Latin and Greek culture, but it is only for people with lots of money to buy education. This makes Latin and Greek hated by most people. In such a society Classics departments of universities will find their staff and students are usually from expensive, posh public schools. They may offer Latin to beginners, but at 'ordinary' schools children have probably been educated to think that Latin is not for them. 'Will it help me get a job?'

Actually, the sort of detailed arranging tasks involved in learning Latin, combined with the kinds of fundamental questions sparked off by the study of Classical texts, tend to develop in people an enhanced intellectual nimbleness that makes them good at many jobs. Classics seems worthless only to naively utilitarian inquirers. (To refute them in their own terms, I stockpile the fact that the one person I know who was able to study Classics at her local West of Scotland comprehensive school, then to PhD level at university, ended up on secondment to the World Bank; but she studied Classics simply because she liked it.) No one yet has developed an economic metric that shows how much the study of the poetry of Catullus contributes to social cohesion, economic growth or reducing reoffending rates. It just seems to me both daft and sad if we're living in a society where our rulers think that art only matters if it can be proved that it helps keep the streets clean.

George Buchanan and Arthur Johnston will not help keep the streets clean. It is unlikely that our politicians will think them worthy of focus groups, or that they will be required reading in schools. Still, there may be other reasons why we should read them, enjoy their work as poets, and reflect on their place in Scottish and Western culture. Even thinking about them a little leads us to question some of our culture's values, as well as to realise at times how lucky we are to live in our own time rather than in theirs.

Our era seems very harsh for Scottish Classicists. The decline in employment for traditional Classics teachers has surely been as steep as that in traditional heavy industry, if not steeper. Often the few professional Classicists who remain are temperamentally unsuited to militancy, or else keep quiet out of a fear that they may lose the few surviving jobs. In comparison with other workers in 'elite' areas (such as opera), Classicists have remained fairly mute. The height of their protest has tended to be letters to the press. More outspoken activists such as the young Scottish Classicist John Taylor, whose Theatre Odyssey company has presented Classical drama to schools and the general public of all ages in Fife, Glasgow and elsewhere, have had to leave the country to find work in Classics (even though, in Taylor's case, his Theatre Odyssey supporters include distinguished figures from Sir Kenneth Dover to Liz Lochhead and Tony Harrison). Still, however bleak the position of Classics in Scotland may appear, it is worth remembering that no sooner had that eighteenth-century arbiter of taste, Edinburgh University's progressive Professor Hugh Blair, consigned literature in Scots to the dustbin of history than a poet called Robert Burns published his *Poems, Chiefly in the Scottish Dialect.* I don't think writers across Scotland are about to start publishing Latin odes. But 'progressive' educationalists striving to replace Classics with more 'relevant' subjects in Scottish schools of the 1960s and 1970s could never have predicted the astonishing use that would be made of Classical materials by Ian Hamilton Finlay. I am confident that the Classical tradition will continue to be of enduring importance to Scottish poets, writers, thinkers and imaginative artists of all kinds in this third millennium. I hope that soon there will be much fuller parallel text versions of the works of George Buchanan, Arthur Johnston and other Scottish Latin poets which will fuel that 'specifically Scottish cultural inheritance' signalled by Ronald Knox in his Centenary Lecture to the Classical Association of Scotland in 2002 and which W. N. Herbert develops when he fuses Virgil and D. C. Thomson in *The Bumper Book of Troy*. Even if this hope looks just now like a very pious one, there is no point in accepting a few poisonous messages of sympathy. We should fight like hell to make sure, as part of the internationalising of our culture, we keep and enhance in Scotland an ecosystem which ensures that not only is excellent teaching of Classical Studies and Classical languages offered in primary and secondary schools, but also that the more advanced research and development work in Classics has secure bases in our universities, and that writers, artists, composers, film-makers and digital creators are included in new, evolving networks of Classics in Scotland.

* * *

Time, now, to move beyond polemic, to the more important matter of poetry. Time to say more about these two Scottish Renaissance Latin poets and their work. This is a poetry book, not a rant or an antiquarian curiosity. I was first attracted to Buchanan and Johnston because I wanted to make poems, and I thought they might help me to do so. As I made more versions of their poems, I came more and more to appreciate the range and lovely dexterity of their work, so it seemed to me imaginatively appropriate to include poems which showed something of that range, even where I felt compelled to offer something closer to a rendering rather than a fully achieved poem in English. That way, I could at least suggest something of the plenitude of tones and subject matter in each poet. There are maybe under a dozen versions in this book which could stand on their own as decent modern poems, but I hope there is a range of others which will at least convince today's readers that Buchanan and Johnston have something enriching to say.

George Buchanan (1506–1582) and Arthur Johnston (c.1579–1641) are Apollos of the North. Hugh MacDiarmid thought them 'among the greatest poets Scotland has produced'. Renaissance men, they benefited from the way Renaissance scholarship and art were able to reconnect Europe with the ancient culture of the Classics. 'Humanity' is the old term for Latin in the Scottish universities (Glasgow University still has a 'Humanity Classroom'), and the humane scholars who reinvestigated Classical culture in the Renaissance, taking it out of the confines of monasteries and universities in order to put it at the service of the *res publica*, politics, courts and princes, were called Humanists. Out of Humanism, spurred by the study of Classical languages, came a resurgent European cultural flowering. In Scotland this was evident in the late fifteenth and early sixteenth centuries in works like the translation of Virgil's *Aeneid* into Scots by Gavin Douglas, Bishop of Dunkeld, and in such building projects as the extension of Falkland Palace in Fife or the founding of King's College, Aberdeen. The founder of King's, Bishop William Elphinstone, had been educated at the universities of Glasgow, Paris and Orleans, and treasured in his library a copy of the influential Italian Humanist Lorenzo Valla's *De Elegantia Latinae Linguae*. George Buchanan would also own a copy of this book, and, like Arthur Johnston after him, would regard his own work as contributing to European culture.

Buchanan's European contemporaries include Titian (whose great 1559 Classical painting of Diana and Actaeon now hangs in the National Gallery of Scotland), as well as the Dutch Humanist Catholic Classical scholar Erasmus who flyted in Latin with Germany's Protestant Martin Luther. Later, Arthur Johnston was a contemporary of the Italian composer Monteverdi (whose operas include the Classical *Orfeo* of 1607 and *Il Ritorno d'Ulisse* (1641)) as well as of William Shakespeare, dramatist of *Titus Andronicus* (1594), *Julius Caesar* (1599), *Coriolanus* (c.1607) and other plays set in the Classical world. Classics made the Renaissance, and the Renaissance in turn liked to view itself in a Classical mirror.

Scots who spent a good deal of their lives in continental Europe, Buchanan and Johnston enjoyed, in their lifetimes and for long after, high reputations across the Western world of the Renaissance and Enlightenment. Though neither of these men is a Michelangelo or a Shakespeare, each was rightly regarded as a poet of quality. In his essay 'On the Education of Children' Michel de Montaigne, who had been taught by Buchanan in Bordeaux, described his former dominie as 'the great Scottish poet'. Another contemporary, Henri Estienne, called him 'easily the leading poet of his era'. Renaissance kings, scholars and teachers relished Buchanan's poetry, whether they read it in Portugal or Poland, Germany, France, Italy, Scotland or England. Arthur Johnston, Buchanan's most fervent Scottish admirer, was too young ever to have met his literary hero, but sang his praises and won an admiring audience for his own poetry in Germany, Italy, Holland, the nations of Britain, and beyond. In the eighteenth century, Samuel Johnson (an accomplished poet in Latin as well as English) regarded Johnston as one of Scotland's finest poets, and the leading Scottish Latin poet, after Buchanan.

The Renaissance milieu of which George Buchanan and Arthur Johnston were part was rich in artists (from Albrecht Dürer to Michelangelo) who loved the Classical world, and was dominated by imperial powers such as Spain and Portugal which sought empires as large as Rome's, but Europe was also riven by violent conflicts. Many of these centred round the Protestant Reformation, that movement by some Christians to revise modes of worship, and to throw off papal authority and perceived abuses of Church power. Sixteenth-century Scotland, despite its size, played an important part in this Reformation. Continental Europe was dominated by the Hapsburg Holy Roman Empire, centred on Austria but with a branch of the Catholic Hapsburg royal family also controlling the throne of Spain. As the Protestant Reformation, encouraged by the great Catholic Classicist Erasmus, grew in Germany, religious warfare proliferated across Europe, complicating other dynastic and territorial rivalries. In England King Henry VIII, having invaded France in 1512 and crushed the Scots at the Battle of Flodden in 1513, broke with the Roman Catholic Church in the mid-1530s and became head of the Protestant English Church. Across Europe, Protestants were fought by Catholic forces – most virulently as the Inquisition developed. Conflicts were felt not only in nations but within institutions such as the universities. This was certainly the case in the universities of St Andrews and Paris where George Buchanan was a student in the 1520s – several decades before, around 1560, the Scottish Reformation fully ignited with the extremely active encouragement of John Knox.

In France, Scotland's traditional ally, the Roman Catholic Guise family, warred with the Protestant Bourbons in the mid-sixteenth century. France had a substantial Huguenot Protestant minority, and the French aspired to link with and control Scotland in order to curb growing English power. Many Scots were Francophiles, though after the Catholic Mary, Queen of Scots fled to seek the protection of Queen Elizabeth in England in 1568, the Scottish King James VI became more inclined towards England, and eventually succeeded the childless Elizabeth on the English throne in 1603, uniting the crowns of Scotland and England. Before long, though, the seventeenth century saw the outbreak in Europe of the Thirty Years War (1618–1648), again a struggle involving Protestant and Catholic ideologies. The shocks and aftershocks of these European struggles are often sensed in the poetry of Buchanan and Johnston, so that these writers seem, on occasion, mirrors of their times. Nonetheless, in their poetry they were not social commentators but creative artists whose appeal remains aesthetic, not merely historical.

However remarkable their poetry, and however distinguished they were in earlier centuries, the repression of Classics in the Scottish educational system and the minimal or very selective approach to Scottish literature pursued outside Scotland mean that these poets are very little known today. Buchanan is remembered, if at all, as a political thinker rather than as a poet, while even among professional Latinists the name of Arthur Johnston is often unknown. This is the first volume ever to bring together substantial selections from both poets' work for the modern reader, and it makes sense to outline who these two poets were.

Buchanan first: he was born around the start of February 1506 at a farm called The Moss, near Killearn in Stirlingshire, probably to a family who spoke Gaelic. Though the thatched cottage in which Buchanan was born is now demolished, an obelisk to his memory was erected nearby in 1788 at the height of the Scottish Enlightenment. The fifth of eight children, Buchanan was brought up substantially by his mother since his father died when George was aged about six. Buchanan's maternal uncle, James Heriot, seems to have encouraged the teenager to go to Paris when he was fourteen, but Heriot's death led to Buchanan's return to Scotland. At seventeen Buchanan served as a soldier with the French army that helped the Scots beat off an English invasion force sent to Scotland by Henry VIII. Then with his brother Patrick he enrolled for a short time as a student at the University of St Andrews. A contemporary there was the Dundonian John Wedderburn (c.1505–1556) who later helped his brothers make the Scots collection *The Gude and Godlie Ballatis* which followed Martin Luther and attacked 'The Paip, that Pagane full of pryde'. Another of Buchanan's St Andrews contemporaries was Patrick Hamilton who wrote Lutheran theology in Latin and was burned as a heretic in front of St Salvator's College, St Andrews, on the orders of Archbishop James Beaton, in 1528. Buchanan went to St Andrews to study with the philosopher and historian John Major (sometimes called John Mair), and graduated with a BA in 1525. Though Buchanan wrote later that his teacher was 'major in name only', he followed his professor in several beliefs, including the idea that monarchs might be subject to the will of their people. Certainly Buchanan followed John Major to the University of Paris, and continued his studies there in 1527. In Renaissance Paris Buchanan studied not only Latin but also Greek, from which he went on to make Latin translations of poets as different as Simonides and Euripides. Influential at this time were the writings of the French Classicist Guillaume Budé who stressed, as Buchanan's modern biographer I. D. McFarlane puts it, 'the great relevance of the classical world to contemporary existence'.

At the University of Paris Buchanan studied Latin verse composition. He later went on to teach at a Parisian college. He owned works such as Terentius Morus's 1510 study of Latin prosody, which he later presented to the University of St Andrews. This book explained the many metres and styles of ancient Latin poetry, most of which had been ignored in the late Middle Ages. Buchanan became a master of the Latin verse forms set out by Morus. In the first book of his own *Elegies* he writes lively Latin poetry about student life (yells, beatings), and mentions poets he studied such as Virgil, Ovid and the first-century court poet Statius. Buchanan's copy of Statius, with what are probably his own marginalia in Latin and Greek, is now in the Special Collections Department of St Andrews University Library, bound together with Lorenzo Valla's Humanist treatise on the Latin language. Buchanan relished Classical rhetoric, and his poems enjoy formal rhetorical display of the sort he would have read in the opening lines of Statius's *Thebaid* (which he annotated). Where Statius titled a gathering of his shorter poems 'Silvae' (literally 'pieces of wood' or 'raw materials' – a title indicating occasional poems which were supposedly hastily composed) Buchanan followed suit, though he aimed to produce short epigrammatic Latin poems of poise and eloquence in the admired Renaissance manner. Buchanan's copy of Statius also includes a substantial manuscript section (with poems) in an educated Humanist hand. It is emblematic of the way books and manuscript material circulated among Buchanan's Humanist network. In Paris the Scottish poet was part of a circle of neo-Latin and French poets and teachers. Some of Buchanan's early work was translated into French by the poet Joachim Du Bellay. Poetic genres such as the *pasquil* or *pasquinade* (a satiric poetry linked with the Roman statue of Pasquino, and directed against the Popes) and the neo-Latin paraphrase of the Hebrew Psalms were becoming popular in this period, and would be taken up by Buchanan. His 'dearest' friend the polylingual Elgin-born neo-Latin poet Florence Wilson (c.1504–1547), seems to have given Buchanan a 1523 Hebrew Dictionary around this time in Paris.

In the early 1530s Buchanan worked as tutor to a young Scottish nobleman, Gilbert Kennedy, Earl of Cassilis, with whom he had returned to Scotland by 1536. Back in Scotland he wrote a Latin dream ('Somnium') poem which started off by translating a Scots poem by the great Makar, William Dunbar (c.1460–c.1520):

> This nycht befoir the dawing cleir   *dawn*
> Me thocht Sanct Francis did to me appeir,
> With ane religious abbeit in his hand,   *habit*
> And said, 'In this go cleieth the my servand.   *clothe; servant*
> Reffus the warld, for thow mon be a freir.   *Refuse; friar*

The young Buchanan never took holy orders. Though he later told the Inquisition in Portugal that his 'Somnium' was simply 'translating an old Scots epigram into Latin verse', he went far beyond Dunbar in satirising the Franciscan order of monks, and he went even further in his extended satire 'Franciscanus', part of which appears in the present selection under the English-language title 'The Exorcist'. In the 'Franciscanus', Buchanan drew on Virgil, on the satirists Juvenal and Persius, and on later Latin poets such as Claudian, Statius and Lucan; yet this energetic extended poem also winks towards Horace, Martial and others. With its fancy Greek derivations (in a name like 'Caecodaemon') and its many Classical echoes, 'Franciscanus' even more than the 'Somnium' is a tour de force. The Scottish King James V encouraged Buchanan to write these poems, which helped the King appease anticlerical sentiments in Scotland, at the same time as James stopped short of following Henry VIII in breaking with the Church of Rome. Other Scottish poets associated with the royal court also drew on European Humanist writings (such as those of Erasmus) to question the power of the priesthood; one such poet in Scots was Sir David Lindsay of the Mount, whom Buchanan knew, and whose 1552 verse play *Ane Satyre of the Thrie Estaitis* may be read alongside the 'Franciscanus' and others of Buchanan's Reformation poems. Buchanan, however, went beyond Lindsay in his open support for Protestantism and, later, his sometimes furious denunciations of papal power.

    This tendency got him into serious trouble. Scottish anti-heresy laws had been renewed in 1535, and show-trials of heretics were not uncommon. Buchanan feared that Cardinal David Beaton, Archbishop of St Andrews and nephew of the James Beaton who had burned Patrick Hamilton, wanted to put him on trial, but King James V appears to have helped the poet escape to England in early 1539. Buchanan may well have been in mortal danger; David Beaton had the Classicist and Lutheran preacher George Wishart burned at St Andrews in 1546 before Beaton himself was assassinated by Protestants.

    From London, Buchanan went to France, and a teaching post at the Collège de Guyenne in Bordeaux. This post was offered to him by the Portuguese Humanist André de Gouvea. The college teaching involved a thorough immersion in the Classics, and Latin verse composition. For its young male pupils (who included Montaigne) Buchanan wrote his own Latin plays *Baptistes* (a political drama about John the Baptist) and *Jephthes* (a powerful, disturbing tragedy about loyalty to God), as well as translating Euripides's *Medea* and *Alcestis* from Greek into Latin. The boys of the school acted in *Baptistes* in 1542, and in *Medea* the following year. These plays are important in the evolution of French theatre and were known in Britain. Though we have no record of their being performed in Renaissance Scotland, it is notable that several Scottish editions were published in Latin (with other works by Buchanan) during the Scottish Enlightenment, and an English prose translation of *A Tragedy of Jephthah, or, The Vow* was made by William Tait, 'School-master in Drummelzier', and published in 1750 at the start of the major revival in Scottish playwriting headed by the Reverend John Home, author of the tragedy *Douglas* (1756). It was no doubt helpful, at a time when many Kirk people considered the theatre scandalous, to have a reminder that the great Protestant Buchanan had written what Tait called such an 'edifying and diverting' drama. If the Scottish Enlightenment looked to Buchanan's plays, so did the twentieth-century Scottish Renaissance, when Robert Garioch published his Scots translations of *Jephthah and the Baptist* in 1959.

Buchanan's Latin dramas were written in France, but the work which made him most famous as a poet is associated with his time in Portugal. The Portuguese King João III invited André de Gouvea to become Principal of the university in the ancient medieval cathedral city of Coimbra in 1547. Buchanan went with him, but soon found himself writing an epitaph for his boss and friend, when de Gouvea, the Portuguese Humanist who was eager to improve learning in his native land, died a year later. The elegant opening words of Buchanan's verse epitaph ('Gouvea, you gave so much and got so little') show his clear admiration for this man of letters. Buchanan wrote a good deal of secular and satirical poetry in Portugal, including bawdy poems about a bawd and her daughter, Leonora; in these poems he does not mince his words, and can seem misogynistic. While he could write impressively and sycophantically about the Portuguese King, Buchanan could be deeply suspicious of the unfettered pursuit of imperial wealth which he often saw as characterising Portuguese ambitions. He denounced the Portuguese colonisation of Brazil, and wrote a poem called 'In Polyonymum' which clearly and dangerously mocks the Portuguese monarch's grandiosity – hardly a safe thing to do.

After André de Gouvea's death there were problems in the college at Coimbra where Buchanan taught for a time along with his brother Patrick, also a Humanist scholar. Academic jealousies, suspicions of heresy, corruption – all simmered for a few years until the Catholic Inquisitor-General launched an investigation into the attitudes and conduct of several members of staff. Buchanan was convinced at this time that he was 'shopped' to the Inquisition by one of his colleagues, Belchior Beleago, for whom he had an intense dislike. Beleago appears to have been a scholar of Greek, shifty, with a ruthless eye for his own financial advantage, and ready to spread malicious rumours about heresy, though Buchanan (a man reputed to have a quarrelsome temper) no doubt exaggerated Beleago's vices to enhance the power of the invective in the poems he wrote against this colleague. These poems make no secret of an antisemitic strain visible in Buchanan's work. Buchanan's poetry can draw on the prejudices of his age (from homophobia to antisemitism) and indeed concentrate them to intensify a strain of Juvenalian invective which is most obvious in his Reforming denunciations of the papacy and popish practices. It is not necessary to share Buchanan's views in order to relish the force of his poetry.

Buchanan was arrested, confined and interrogated by the Inquisition in Portugal between August 1550 and January 1551. His rooms and private papers were searched. One book taken from him (and later returned) was his copy of Stifel's *Arithmetica integra*, a Latin mathematics text, which Buchanan later presented to the University of St Andrews. It is in excellent condition, and still inside its back cover is an ink note, written presumably by an officer of the Inquisition, recording that the book has been taken from 'Jorge bucanano'. Few artefacts are more redolent of Buchanan's career than this one. Its survival is testimony both to the extreme danger Buchanan faced several times in his career, and to how attached he was to his books.

In the hands of the Inquisition, Buchanan was very, very frightened. He was terrified that the 'Franciscanus' and 'Somnium' might be held against him, along with other breaches of Church regulations, and that (especially if Cardinal Beaton's resentment caught up with him) he might face execution for heresy. During and after a period of imprisonment he worked on his Latin paraphrase of the Hebrew Old Testament Psalms, regarded in the Renaissance as his greatest production. Buchanan often revised these paraphrases over a number of years, but for modern readers the most arresting moment in them is surely the start of his paraphrase of Psalm XXIII. In the Renaissance English translation authorised by King James VI and I, this famous psalm begins gently, 'The Lord is my shepherd; I shall not want'. Buchanan's paraphrase, however, opens totally differently, in the midst of threatened violence:

Quid frustra rabidi me petitis, canes?
Livor, propositum cur premis improbum?

Rabid dogs, why waste your time on me?
Envy, why carry on with your corruption?

These sentiments surely relate to his time at the hands of the Inquisition, and, while it is very difficult to represent in English any of Buchanan's Latin Psalm paraphrases (since we have our own versions of the Psalms in English already), I have tried in this book to make a version of Buchanan's Psalm XXIII which is alert to his circumstances at the hands of the Inquisition, and to his determined longing for God's protection and consolation.

Buchanan's Psalm paraphrases were not published until the mid-1560s (when, in a beautiful poem, he dedicated them to Mary, Queen of Scots), but they were received as a masterpiece, and fuse Biblical Hebraic with Classical poetic effects, glancing particularly towards the Odes of Horace. For a modern audience they may be most beautiful not when read as texts, but if heard sung to the 1579 settings made by Buchanan's younger contemporary the Geneva-based French composer Jean Servin (Johannes Servinus, c.1530–c.1596) who dedicated his settings to King James VI of Scotland, whom he addressed in a Latin preface that praises the dignity, splendour and elegance of Buchanan's Psalm paraphrases. I. D. McFarlane reported that 'In Lord Amherst's Library, there is said to be a copy bound with the arms of James VI of Scotland', and it is likely that this poet-king (who liked to pattern himself on the psalmist King David, and who was tutored by Buchanan, then went on to make his own paraphrases of Psalms) would have valued a copy of the book. Servin emphasised that his music owed nothing to the contemporary popular taste for soft and artificial melody; instead, his motet-like work is rich and full, employing between four and eight voices. His setting of Buchanan's paraphrase of Psalm XXIII has music in four parts, and his technique often involves setting a word or syllable in 'an aureole of sound, radiating in the splendour of melodic glories'. So wrote George Bell in his 'Notes on Some Music Set to Buchanan's Paraphrase of the Psalms' in 1906, where he reproduces Servin's music for Psalm XXIII. Though Servin's 1579 work is now very rare (there is a copy in the Library of Trinity College, Dublin), it would surely appeal to modern ears if recorded on CD, and would form a complement to the magnificent Scottish Mass settings of Robert Carver composed earlier in the sixteenth century and recorded in 1991 by Capella Nova.

Fortunately, Buchanan's Psalm paraphrases were not his last work. The Inquisition spared his life, and sentenced him instead to a period of re-education. After a considerable number of interrogations his Inquisitors informed Buchanan on 29 July 1551 that he had been found guilty of believing that the body of Christ was present only figuratively in the Sacrament; of believing that justification was by faith only and that confession was a human rather than a divine invention; of believing that minor lawbreaking was permissible if it caused no harm; and of other doubts and hesitations. They noted that he preferred to pray directly to God, rather than seeking the intercession of the Saints. However, he was asked to renounce his errors in public, was placed under house arrest for a time, where he was to perform exercises to help save his soul, and he had his excommunication officially withdrawn. Compared with what he feared might happen, Buchanan had got off lightly. He was lucky.

What Buchanan wanted to do now was to get out of Portugal. It is likely that he had already written his poem of longing for Paris, the 'Desiderium Lutetiae', which seems to express strong personal feelings, even if the girls in this poem by a man who never married may represent merely competing intellectual factions imploring him to stay in Portugal rather than go to the Paris represented by his 'Amaryllis'. First of all he went for a few months to London, but it was Paris that drew him in late 1552, and his poem 'Adventus in Galliam', called in the version in this present book 'Coming to France', is a celebration of many of the things Buchanan loved in French culture. For the next few years he relished conversing with leading French poets, scholars and aristocrats. Around 1555 he was given the job of tutor to Timoléon de Cossé, a young French nobleman, and divided his time between northern Italy and France, especially Paris. Though Buchanan was not in holy orders, he was given an allowance – the prebend of Mulleville in Coutances Cathedral by Timoléon's grateful family in 1558. As part of the schooling of his tutee Buchanan began his long verse exposition of the geography and make-up of the earth, *De Sphaera*, a poem whose science is (and in important, anti-Copernican ways *was* even in its own day) outdated, but which is also a hymn to the scientific intellect, the exploring mind. *De Sphaera* was partly modelled on the thirteenth-century treatise on the earth *De Sphaera Mundi* by the Paris-based English Latinist Sacrobosco (John Halifax), who had drawn on Greek and Arabic texts. Buchanan worked on his *De Sphaera* intermittently throughout the rest of his life, but never completed it. The sections in the present selection which set out his aims and hymn scientific minds of the past show the amplitude of his Renaissance vision. Buchanan, like Milton, was a poet preoccupied with knowledge, and at his best used his preoccupation to nourish rather than clog his poetry. So, for instance, though his horse poem 'De Equo Elogium' was written by a man who came from a horse culture and who (as a one-time soldier) would have seen horses in battle, as Philip J. Ford points out it also draws on the lines of Virgil and on hints from other Latin poets quoted in the entry for 'equus' (horse) in the 1518 edition of Ravisius Textor's *Spicimen epithetorum* which thematically arranges snippets of Classical poetry of the sort that appealed to Renaissance epigrammatists. Like Milton, MacDiarmid, Auden and many other poets, Buchanan loved dictionaries, information and lists, building all into his poetry.

Cultured and cosmopolitan, Buchanan felt wholly at home in France, as well he might. In 1548 Mary Stewart, daughter of Scotland's King James V, had been betrothed, according to the Treaty of Haddington, to the French Dauphin, Francis of Valois. The same treaty had conceded to France's King Henry II the role of protector of Scotland, giving him oversight of Scottish civil, military and diplomatic business. Mary of Guise was appointed Regent of Scotland in 1554. For a Euro-Scot like Buchanan, the prospect of 1550s Scotland as a French protectorate would have been welcome, and it is no surprise that Buchanan took French nationality, hymned France with patriotic love ('patrio . . . amore') in 'Coming to France', and delighted in the company of many French poets who wrote in both Latin and French. Though we may often think of older Europe as riven by nationalistic strife, the Latin literary communities of countries such as France (and, to a lesser degree, Scotland) were impressively multicultural and cosmopolitan. Latin was a language which let scholars, poets and others who used it travel widely. This was not quite the modern European Community's Europe without borders, but the Europe of the Latinists made for transnational literary allegiances, even at times when nations might be at war.

It was an age, like any other, of political intrigue. As Roger Mason writes in his 'Renaissance and Reformation' chapter in Jenny Wormald's *Scotland. A History* (2005):

> Some weeks before the marriage of Mary and Francis in April 1558, the Scottish queen had signed a 'secret' document bequeathing her kingdom to the French crown should there be no children of the marriage. Together with the Scottish parliament's bestowal of the crown matrimonial on Francis in November 1558, this bound Scotland in perpetuity to the French monarchy, a provincial outpost of the expanding Valois empire. To the prospect of uniting the French and Scottish crowns, moreover, was added the possibility of ousting Elizabeth from the English throne in favour of Mary Stewart's Catholic claim.

These were the political circumstances in which Buchanan, perhaps the most Francophile among many Francophile Scottish writers, produced his great 'Epithalamium' or wedding hymn celebrating the marriage of Mary, Queen of Scots to Francis of Valois, the Dauphin. This is one of Buchanan's major works, and the longest poem included in the present selection. Only the 936-line 'Franciscanus' and the five-book *De Sphaera* exceed it in length. With its verbal repetitions and formal praise, Buchanan's 'Epithalamium' manages to be both elegantly amplitudinous and forcefully argued, with flashes of lyric happiness and expectation. It is assured and appropriately majestic, while avoiding being merely formulaic. If his praise of the monarchs is at times predictable, deftly impressive and more original is his extended paean to Scotland, details of which draw on the Latin *Scotorum historia a prima gentis origine* (History of the Scots from the First Origin of the People) written by Hector Boece, Principal of the University of Aberdeen. Boece's history was first published in Paris in 1527. Buchanan ends his poem with a ringing hope that Scotland and France may be bonded together as part of a coming greater union 'Aequava aeternis coeli concordia flammis' (Tuned to the timeless concord of the stars). Yet within the poem he has been careful to outline the unique history of Scotland and sing its praises in a way designed to ensure its distinctiveness remains fully articulated.

Within a few years of writing this 'Epithalamium', Buchanan was back in Scotland. A letter of 7 April 1562 records how he read Livy with Mary, Queen of Scots to whom he acted at times as a tutor. On the death of France's King Henry II in 1559, Mary had been proclaimed Queen of France, when her feeble fifteen-year-old husband Francis became King. Francis died in 1560, and the Catholic Mary left behind the political infighting and religious warfare of France to return to Scotland in 1561 at the height of the Scottish Reformation. In 1560, Scotland's Reformation Parliament had repudiated the Pope, outlawed the Mass, and adopted Protestantism as the state religion. Though Buchanan got on well enough with John Knox, his poetry manifests a clear admiration for Mary, Queen of Scots in her girlhood and young womanhood. Mary was herself a poet and supporter of poets. When Buchanan styles her 'Nympha' (nymph) he uses a term of address not unusual in Renaissance Latin poems admiring young women, but his decision to dedicate his Psalm paraphrases to her, and the tone of his dedicatory poem to her contrast markedly with Knox's much more wranglingly aggressive attitude. Though he would later defend the deposition of Mary as Queen, Buchanan was a sympathetic and trusted intellectual guide around the time when she and he first returned to Scotland.

Recognised as a Humanist of international standing, Buchanan was also involved in such tasks as the interpretation for the Queen and Scottish Privy Council of legal documents written in Spanish, French, Latin and English.

He participated in an institutional review of the University of St Andrews in 1562. Among other things, this was designed to strengthen the teaching of Latin and Greek in the Arts college, with Hebrew in Divinity, and made clear that the students were to take part in Latin rhetorical contests and open competitions for Latin verse composition. Eventually, Buchanan was appointed Principal of St Leonard's College, St Andrews (part of the University there) in 1566. At St Andrews, then, as now, a centre of creative writing, Buchanan mentored several Scottish Latin poets including David Hume of Godscroft and Hercules Rollock; he was succeeded by another Latin poet, Patrick Adamson. All these Latin poets would be anthologised by Arthur Johnston in the following century.

Though a significant public figure, Buchanan, while he had escaped the Portuguese Inquisition, was clearly aware he lived in troubled times in Scotland. The English versions of the poems in this book have been designed to be freestanding without footnotes, but often the Latin originals are both embroiled in and enriched by a knowledge of the politics of the time. So, for instance, Buchanan's beautifully and fragilely balanced quatrain 'To Henry Darnley, King of Scots' seems to date from the time after the Roman Catholic marriage ceremony in which Darnley wed Mary, Queen of Scots in 1565 and a commemorative medal was struck bearing the inscription *Rex Scottorum* (King of Scots). In February 1566, Darnley was invested in the French Order of St Michael and, after a solemn Mass, proclaimed he had returned Scotland to the 'true faith'. Mary, however, denied Darnley the crown matrimonial and the royal authority that went with it. So in March Darnley joined the Protestant plotters against Mary who stabbed to death her Italian secretary David Riccio in a small chamber at Holyrood Palace in Edinburgh. Buchanan's poem, whose title 'Ad Henricum Scotorum Regem' (To Henry King of Scots) may allude to the commemorative medal, brilliantly catches the dangerous, trembling uncertainty of the times, and comes from a poet familiar with reverses of fortune:

> Caltha suos nusquam vultus a sole reflectit,
>   Illo oriente patens, illo abeunte latens:
> Nos quoque pendemus de te, sol noster, ad omnes
>   Expositi rerum te subeunte vices.

> The marigold nowhere turns from the sun.
> Opening at dawn, it closes in the dusk.
> We too depend on you, our sun. To all
> Your turns of fortune we are left exposed.

Often subsequent events have added pathos as well as irony to Buchanan's poems, but they still speak directly of the strong, even desperate political (and occasionally personal) hopes of the period. So, reading poems such as 'Mutuus Amor' in which Buchanan writes of the unbreakable bond between the Queens Mary and Elizabeth, or the measured verse epistle to Elizabeth's senior courtier, Buchanan's friend Lord Walter Haddon, we appreciate with hindsight that political anxiety may underlie and even at times disrupt the formal surface of Buchanan's poetry. An intense awareness of sudden changes of fortune, as well as an admiration for the superbly shaped pithiness of Simonides's verses, may have been what attracted Buchanan to make several Latin versions of poems attributed to that ancient Greek poet. Like Buchanan's translations of Euripides from Greek into Latin, these versions remind us how much Latin was a widespread living literary language in his day. While many educated readers would not have known Greek, almost all would have been able to read Simonides in Buchanan's Latin. Latin, after all, was the language into which King James VI and I would have his own works translated so that all Europe (and all posterity) might read them.

However Francophile Buchanan was, he had good friends in the English court. These included Roger Ascham (1515–1568), who had tutored Queen Elizabeth before she came to the throne, and was a distinguished writer in Latin and English on topics from archery to translation and education. Ascham admired Buchanan's *Jephthes*, and Buchanan met him in London in 1568; on 20 November that year at Hampton Court Ascham presented Buchanan with a recent edition of Virgil, writing in the book that he gave it 'Anglus Scoto, amicus amico' (as an Englishman to a Scotsman, a friend to a friend) and that just as Virgil was the greatest of the ancient poets, so Buchanan was the greatest of the modern age. Buchanan's Latin version of Euripides's *Alcestis* had been performed at Court in front of Queen Elizabeth on an earlier occasion. The Classically-educated Queen was herself a Latin author. She is said to have been so moved by the theme of Buchanan's play – the sacrifice of a woman who offers to die instead of her husband – that she asked for the whole performance to be repeated. The English Queen made the famous observation 'Buchananum omnibus antepono. Haddonum nemini postpono' (I rank Buchanan before all the rest, and Haddon second to none). This tactful remark showed favour both to Buchanan and to another of his English literary friends, the Latin poet, friend of Ascham, and lawyer-courtier Lord Walter Haddon (1516–1572). Buchanan's 1564 verse epistle to Haddon is at once formal and relaxed, dignified, affectionate and politically purposeful. In elegance and self-mockery its tone seems to anticipate some of the English poetry of Classicist Ben Jonson, though it predates his birth by almost a decade. Buchanan's presentation of himself as a sort of grey-haired Apollo is endearing, and should be kept in mind when reading some of his more vituperative, sectarian poems. Like the Scottish poet William Dunbar, whose work he seems to have admired, Buchanan is a poet of impressive tonal and thematic variety, an archer with many strings to his bow.

By the late 1560s, he was nimble in ideology as well as verse. Buchanan seems to have turned against Mary, Queen of Scots around the time when, very soon after the murder of Darnley, she married his murderer the Earl of Bothwell in 1567. In that crucial year Buchanan served as Moderator of the General Assembly of the Church of Scotland, the most distinguished poet ever to do so. He helped negotiate the Assembly's support for the Regent Moray whose army defeated Mary's at the Battle of Langside, Glasgow, on 13 May 1568. This defeat precipitated the Queen's flight to England where she threw herself on the mercy of Elizabeth – a decision that eventually led to Mary's execution in 1587, five years after Buchanan's death. Buchanan was involved in the scrutinising of Mary's potentially treacherous conduct, and wrote about it at length in his prose. His presence in London and at Hampton Court in 1568 was linked to Mary's trial. All this surely adds to rather than detracts from the power of those earlier poems in which his admiration for the young Mary is so manifest.

It may have been around the time he was Moderator of the Kirk that Buchanan began work on what is now his famous prose book, *De Iure Regni apud Scotos Dialogus* (A Dialogue on the Law of Kingship among the Scots), though this was not published until 1579, when it appeared in Edinburgh. One of its most striking features is its support for the doctrine of popular sovereignty – that the monarch is an instrument of the people, and that true power belongs to the people rather than the king or queen; this means that in extreme cases the people have the right to get rid of their monarch. Grounded in Classical Stoicism and ideas of *pietas*, as well as owing something to Calvinist resistance theory and the Humanist 'advice to princes' tradition, the *De Iure* is in line with other literary works by Buchanan, such as the *Baptistes*, whose theme is resistance to tyranny, and the outspoken poem against Sulla in the present book. In espousing this doctrine of popular sovereignty, Buchanan followed his old St Andrews teacher John Major. The *De Iure* may be placed in an impressive line which runs from the Declaration of Arbroath through such works as *Ane Satyre of the Thrie Estaitis*, or the seventeenth-century Protestant *Lex Rex* by Samuel Rutherford, and culminates in the republican strain heard in Robert Burns and much vernacular Scottish literature. A shrewd modern edition (with Latin and English on facing pages) was produced by Roger A. Mason and Martin S. Smith in 2004.

In the eighteenth century Buchanan's *De Iure* was republished in a seventeenth-century English translation in Philadelphia in 1766 and surely played a part in the intellectual ferment underlying the Americans' rebellion against Britain's royal rule. George Reid, Presiding Officer of the current Scottish Parliament, recalls that Donald Dewar, shortly before becoming Scotland's First Minister and around the time of the opening of the Scottish Parliament in 1999, was fascinated by Buchanan's doctrine of popular sovereignty which separates power from the person who wields it (as Buchanan puts it in the *De Iure*). In a public lecture at the 2005 Edinburgh International Book Festival, Reid recalled how Donald Dewar had retired from a Glasgow party in the late 1990s and was found hunched over a translation of the *De Iure*. It was striking that when the Queen opened the Scottish Parliament in 1999 though the Scottish crown jewels were present at the ceremony, she did not wear them: a perfect emblem, perhaps, of Buchanan's popular sovereignty.

Like several other Scottish Latin poets, Buchanan wrote a long poem on the birth of Mary's son, the future King James VI, in 1566. It sets out in Roger Mason's words 'an austere vision of kingship and civic responsibility that contrasts starkly – and pointedly – with the elaborate monarchical cult of honour promoted by the queen herself'. When, some years after, Buchanan became the tutor to the young prince, his tutee often reacted against his teaching. Indeed, James's resolute vindication of the divine right of kings can be seen as a determined reaction against Buchanan's politics and political teaching. Later in the seventeenth century, after the Restoration of the British monarchy in the wake of the Cromwellian Republic, Buchanan's *De Iure* was banned by the Privy Council in Scotland in 1664, and in 1683 his works along with those of the great English republican poet John Milton were publicly burned in Oxford: a strange fate for the poet who had praised Mary, Queen of Scots, had been appointed Keeper of the Privy Seal of Scotland, and who had served as tutor to King James VI and I. Nevertheless, it was an understandable fate for this poet whose substantial prose history of Scotland, the *Rerum Scoticarum Historia* (first published in Edinburgh in 1582, before the King's Scottish Parliament of 1584 ordered copies of it to be recalled), again presented the doctrine of popular sovereignty and was dedicated to the young monarch he was teaching, James. Reprinted in Latin at least five times in Scotland in the eighteenth century, and available in abbreviated and translated form, Buchanan's would be a standard history used in Scottish schools for centuries. It helped mould the democratic Protestant ideology of the nation.

Never a man who enjoyed robust health, though one who had survived many dangers, Buchanan was sometimes prevented by illness from playing a full part in the young king's education (James also had another Classicist tutor called Peter Young). Buchanan trained James in Latin verse composition and in Latin and Greek pronunciation. Sometimes Buchanan taught other students too, including, it is said, the young polymathic Scottish Latin poet James Crichton (1560–1582), recently graduated from St Andrews and soon to head for Italy, death and a huge posthumous reputation as 'the Admirable Crichton'. Buchanan recommended books for the royal library which included works by Ascham, Du Bellay and neo-Latin poets (Buchanan's own Psalm paraphrases were included). Buchanan is said to have beaten the young King, and certainly King James later complained about the 'violence of his humour and heat of his spirit'. In his 1656 *Advice to a Son* Francis Osborn wrote that 'King James used to say of a person in high place about him, that he even trembled at his approach, it minded him so of his pedagogue'. After the death of his old dominie, Buchanan, James seems to have spoken of him with a detestation similar to that James felt for John Knox whose Protestant democratic impulses and whose committed inflexibility the divine-right monarch loathed. However, even James was an admirer of Buchanan as a poet.

The King's admiration was shared by intellectuals across Europe, and not least by the leaders of the Protestant Reformation. Buchanan's remarkable elegy for John Calvin, the French Latinist and Protestant theologian who died in 1564, moves from acute praise into a virulent denunciation of papal abuses. In this poem when he writes of Calvin Buchanan does not go in for elaborate imagery to describe the dead theologian, but, like other Protestant poets, makes remarkable use of imagery to do with light. More warmly friendly is Buchanan's poem to Calvin's French successor, Theodore Bèze (Beza), a friend of several Scottish Latin poets, and a man who, like Buchanan, wrote sometimes risqué Latin poetry in his youth, as well as a later Biblical drama about sacrifice, and, after Calvin's death, led the Genevese church and presided at French synods as Buchanan had presided over the Scottish General Assembly. Thinking of these men as poets, not simply as churchmen, reminds us that Protestantism in Europe (and particularly in the Scotland of Buchanan, the Latin writer and educationalist Andrew Melville, and others) should not be seen as simply anti-artistic. Buchanan's admiration for Beza is evident in his poem to him (included in the present volume), while Beza had known Buchanan since the 1540s, admired his Psalm paraphrases in particular, and regarded the Scotsman as 'the father of literature and especially of Latin poetry'. Beza too published a paraphrase of the Psalms, and he included Buchanan in his

Icones, a collection of accounts of admirable men, dedicated to King James VI. By May 1574 Peter Young, Buchanan's fellow royal tutor (and the future co-translator of King James's works into Latin), was writing to Beza that

> ... D. Buchananus, venerandus senex, quem ego, ut parentem, non immerito obseruo ac colo, consenuit quidem, quod tu doles, sed cruda tamen adhuc satis viridisque senecta: utinam etiam viuax et diuturna! Is te salutat plurimum.
>
> ... Master Buchanan, a venerable old man whom very properly I respect and worship, as if he were my father, has aged to be sure, which you will be sorry to learn; but so far his old age is lively and flourishing. I would like my own old age to be as vigorous and lasting. He sends you many greetings.

Towards the end of his life, during the rule of Regent Morton in Scotland, Buchanan's political prestige slowly waned. He was at work on his history of the nation, and may still have been hoping to complete the *De Sphaera* – both projects that are now linked to his role as educator of the young James VI – but he was writing little or no poetry. Though it is often hard to date his poems precisely, most seem to belong to his early and middle years. Buchanan's work frequently circulated in manuscript, but he published relatively little of his poetry until he was in his sixties. In his lifetime his principal books were his paraphrases of the Psalms (of which full editions appeared from the mid-1560s), *Franciscanus* (1566), and other selections of his poetry in the later 1560s and 1570s. Not until the collected *Poemata* published in Edinburgh several decades after his death by Andrew Hart in 1615, was something like the full range of his poetry readily available in print. Nevertheless, Buchanan's work had circulated sufficiently in manuscript and in printed books that his international reputation was made.

There are relatively few close accounts of the character of this lifelong bachelor, this Renaissance poet-scholar-historian-churchman-dramatist-teacher-translator-administrator-diplomat-politician who could inspire great loyalty among some of his friends and pupils, in awe, perhaps, of his polymathic abilities. Perhaps the best sketch of his character was written by the Scottish nobleman and diarist Sir James Melville of Hallhill:

> Bot Mester George Buchanan was a stoick philosopher, and loked not far before the hand; a man of notable qualities for his learnyng and knawledge in Latin poesie, mekle maid accompt of in other contrees, plaisant in company rehersing at all occasions moralites schort and fecfull [forceful]. He was also of gud religion for a poet, bot he was easely abused and sa facill [easily influenced] that he wes

led with any company that he hanted for the tym, quhilk maid him factious in his auld age, for he spak and met as they that wer about him for the tym infourmed him. For he was becom sleperie and cairles, and folowed in many thingis the vulgair oppinion; for he was naturally populaire, and extrem vengeable against any man that had offendit him, quhilk was his gretest falt. For he wret dispytfull inuectiywes against the Erle of Monteith, for some particulaires that was betwen him and the lard of Buchwhennen; and becam the Erle of Morton's gret ennemy, for ane hackeney of his that chancit to be tane fra his saruand during the ciuill troubles, and was bocht by the Regent.

This reveals several things about the diarist (including his assumption that poets are unlikely to be 'of gud religion'), but gives what seems an insightful account of the temper of the man whose most widely quoted works included the witty epigram on the unidentified 'Zoilus' (in this present volume), and who had written so splenetically about Beleago and about the papacy. Though it may have made him personally difficult at times, a quarrelsome strain in Buchanan enhances and adds sting to his satirical poems.

Buchanan's many anti-papal and anti-Catholic diatribes, *pasquilades*, epigrams and satires should not be seen only in terms of a quarrelsome trait, however. When Buchanan was twenty-one the young Scottish Protestant Patrick Hamilton had been burned to death outside the doors of his St Andrews *alma mater*. In the age of the Inquisition, Buchanan himself had been imprisoned for his beliefs. During this period of religious executions, prisoners of conscience, and constant Church and state surveillance, Buchanan was a rebel against the dominant ecclesiastical power and courts of Europe, those of the Catholic Church. He fought in his writings for what he regarded as religious freedoms, and campaigned against abuses of power. Neither side in the Reformation had unique access to right; both sides had blood on their hands. But Buchanan's 'sectarian' poetry had a heroic and daring urgency; writing in what was the established tongue of the Catholic Church, he sought to attack what he saw as corrupt power, using the very weapons of that power itself. In that sense, his use of Latin may be compared to the way postcolonial writers such as Derek Walcott make use of the English language as well as the Classical tradition. Though Buchanan, the Reformation poet who used an 'elite' language but sided with the 'populaire' and even 'vulgaire', wrote relatively few poems that we might readily call 'spiritual', his virulent campaigning was intended to clear a new space for spiritual belief, one which Buchanan saw as a truer space than that of the Roman Church. He had the courage of deep convictions, and followed through from a position of endangered marginality in Portugal to take the initiative in leading his Kirk in Scotland at the height of the Reformation. His example gives the lie to the notion that Scottish Protestantism and the artistic life need be divorced, and it would be of value to the lively and sometimes uneasy synergy of Kirk and culture in the Scottish Enlightenment.

Though he did write some work in the vernacular, in most of his prose and all his poetry Buchanan used the language of the Romans against Rome. His most intense religious work is probably that of the Latin versions of the Psalms, in which he revoiced scripture for his own age and milieu. When he writes in his own 'original' poetry, he is most often in attack and public mode in dealing with religion, yet there are also indications of the value he placed on pure, inner spiritual experience, as in the concluding lines of 'The Image to the Pilgrims' in the present volume. Protestant Scotland may too often have valued Buchanan for his Protestantism alone: he is a great, brave, and sometimes venomous poet of religious protest, but more than that he is a poet unconfined to one tone or subject matter. Today, without demeaning or patronising the intensity of his Protestant beliefs, we may appreciate the range and skill of his verse as well as his place in religious and political history.

In his last years Buchanan lived in and around Edinburgh. He signed and dated a number of documents from Dalkeith, and tradition has it that he completed his *Historia* in the tower of Sherriffhall House there. Towards the end of his life he had a room in the Palace of Holyroodhouse. His biographer I. D. McFarlane quotes a bill of works from 5 October 1580:

> the slater is to point Holyroodpalace 'from the Eist quarter of the palace fra Maister George Balquhenan's Chalmer Gawell [gable] to the Abbot of Drumfarlingis Gawell Chalmer ...'

Buchanan was correcting the proofs of his *Historia* right up to his death. Though he had a room at Holyrood, he was not well off for a man of his eminence (his wealth at death was around £100). James Melville and others visited him in September 1581, having heard he was ill, and found him in his room teaching the alphabet to his young servant. This story is attractive (and has attracted the contemporary writer James Robertson, who uses it in his sonnet 'George Buchanan') because it is emblematic of this lifelong educator. So is Melville of Hallhill's story that when the printer worried that an incident recorded in Buchanan's *Historia* might offend the King, Buchanan simply looked the printer in the eye and asked, 'Tell me man, giff I have tauld the treuthe?' The printer answered yes, and Buchanan refused to change a word.

Buchanan died on 28 September 1582. He is buried in Canongate Kirkyard, Edinburgh. Though the site of his grave was forgotten, a memorial in the churchyard was erected in 1878, ninety years after the erection of the obelisk at his birthplace. For many, though, Buchanan's greatest memorial was his works, especially as published in two large folio volumes by Thomas Ruddiman in Edinburgh in 1715. Educated at King's College, Aberdeen, Thomas Ruddiman (1674–1757) was a great Latinist and Scottish literary patriot who, in the years immediately following the Union of Parliaments, sought to remind Scots of their rich multilingual literary heritage. So in 1710 he produced an edition of what he regarded as Scotland's greatest work in Scots: the Classicist Gavin Douglas's early Renaissance translation of the *Aeneid*. This was followed in 1711 by the work of Scotland's greatest English-language poet, William Drummond of Hawthornden. Thirdly, and most impressively, Ruddiman edited what has remained to this day the standard edition of Scotland's greatest Latin poet, George Buchanan.

Ruddiman went on to publish the first major poet of the eighteenth-century Scots revival, Burns's admired Allan Ramsay. The editor and printer Ruddiman was one of Scotland's great Latinists, and produced what was until the nineteenth century a standard Latin grammar, his *Rudiments of the Latin Tongue* (1714). His presentation of Buchanan was no more an antiquarian curiosity than was his presentation of Douglas, Drummond or Ramsay. Rather he sought to revitalise Scottish culture through the republishing of literary treasures. His edition of Buchanan was argued over, and Buchanan's work republished, throughout the Scottish Enlightenment, and Buchanan's example should be seen as part of the impetus behind that intellectual era. While Ruddiman's edition of Buchanan was and has remained by far the most celebrated, it was preceded in eighteenth-century Scotland by Robert Monteith's *Very Learned Scotsman, Mr George Buchanan's Fratres Fraterrimi, Three Books of Epigrams, and Book of Miscellanies, in English Verse, with the Illustration of Proper Names, and Mythologies therein mentioned*, published in Edinburgh by Andrew Anderson in 1708. Not only did this work make available a good deal of Buchanan's Latin poetry in English verse translations; it also indicated a continuing modern appetite for Buchanan's work, and probably helped spur Ruddiman's great edition of the originals in Latin. Monteith dedicated his work 'To the Right Honourable, Sir Hugh Dalrymple, of Northberwick, Lord President; and to the Right Honourable Remanent Lords, Senators of the Colledge of Justice'. The College was connected with the Faculty of Advocates in whose library Ruddiman worked in the early years of the eighteenth century. Scots poetry is in Ruddiman's debt.

Buchanan was still a national treasure in the Scottish Enlightenment.

In the early nineteenth century Walter Scott in a note to *Ivanhoe* wrote of 'the celebrated George Buchanan', but despite Victorian memorials, and even the 1871 publication by newsagent John Menzies of a pamphlet of his poems in English translation, Buchanan fell more and more into the hands of academic readers only. Quartercentenary studies appeared in 1906, but Buchanan and the tradition of Latin poetry remained absent from almost all general anthologies of Scottish poetry until the publication of *The New Penguin Book of Scottish Verse* in 2000.

The translations in this present book generally present Buchanan in blank verse, the iambic pentameter form which was the staple of English-language Renaissance poetry and has become the mainstay of formal verse in English. Where English-language poetry relies on stressed beats, Latin poetry relies on vowel lengths, and its quantitative metre is impossible to do justice to in English. Buchanan was a virtuoso master of many Latin verse forms, and I have been unable to represent this aspect of his work. Nonetheless, I have tried at times to suggest verbal dexterity, and I hope that the selection here will do something to convince general readers (who may wish to look across the page at the Latin for a sense of the original sound and frequent beautifully poised word-patterning, enjambment and apposition) that George Buchanan is still alive.

* * *

Arthur Johnston (c.1579–1641) was in no doubt about Buchanan's vitality. Johnston wrote a number of poems championing the older Scottish poet, defended him against detractors, often wrote under his influence, and was a great sustainer and developer of the European and Scottish traditions of which Buchanan was a part. This was recognised by Johnston's contemporaries and immediate successors. In Edinburgh, Andrew Hart, publisher of the first Scottish edition of Buchanan's posthumous 1615 *Poemata*, published four years later the poetic duel between the Scottish Latin poet George Eglishem and the young Arthur Johnston about the quality of Buchanan's work as a psalm translator. If this implies that Hart saw Johnston as the poet best placed to defend Buchanan, then a century later Thomas Ruddiman, after he published his edition of Buchanan's *Opera omnia*, marking the centenary of Hart's edition, went on to edit Johnston's poetic paraphrase of the Song of Solomon in 1729, suggesting that Ruddiman too admired Buchanan first, then Johnston. Arthur's English near-namesake Samuel Johnson was simply revoicing a standard view when, in 1775, writing an account of his tour of Scotland two years earlier, he judged Arthur Johnston to hold 'among the Latin poets of Scotland the next place to the elegant

Buchanan'. By 1814 that omnivorous reader the Classically-trained Walter Scott was writing in chapter XIII of *Waverley* about the ultra-patriotic (and, by nineteenth-century standards, backward-looking) literary tastes of his lovable Lowland Baron Bradwardine who, though his real taste was for prose rather than poetry, nevertheless

> read the classic poets, to be sure, and the Epithalamium of Georgius Buchanan, and Arthur Johnstone's Psalms, of a Sunday; and the Deliciae Poetarum Scotorum, and Sir David Lindsay's Works, and Barbour's Bruce, and Blind Harry's Wallace, and the Gentle Shepherd, and the Cherry and the Slae.

Scott relished Buchanan and Johnston, but knew that they were scarcely in tune with Romantic modernity. By the late nineteenth century Johnston attracted the strong local piety and scholarly acumen of Sir William Duguid Geddes, Principal of the University of Aberdeen, who edited many of Johnston's poems for the Scotophile literary antiquarians of the New Spalding Club. The Latin poet also caught the glancing attention of Hugh MacDiarmid (who published a prose translation of one of Johnston's poems as 'A Fisher's Apology' in his 1940 *Golden Treasury of Scottish Poetry*). However, in modern times Johnston's name is almost unknown: so much so that when I first published versions of a few of his poems around 2000, some people thought I had made him up. Since then, in Polygon's *The Book of St Andrews* (2005), Seamus Heaney, after reading my version of 'To Robert Baron', has presented his poem 'To the Poets of St Andrews' as 'adapted from the lost original "Ut in Lusitania olim miles..." attributed to Arthur Johnston'. Engagingly, Heaney did make this up.

Arthur Johnston was born around 1579 at what was then called Caskieben (later renamed Keithhall), near Inverurie, in Aberdeenshire. He took considerable pride in his birthplace, as poems in the present volume demonstrate. At Inverurie in the winter of 1307–8 King Robert the Bruce had defeated the pro-English forces; not far off from Inverurie was the battlefield of Harlaw where in 1411 Highland clans were comprehensively beaten by a Lowland army headed by Alexander Stewart, Earl of Mar. The Johnstons may have been distantly related to that Earldom. Certainly, Arthur had a sense of himself as coming from classic ground, with which his family had long connections, and where he also acquired his first grounding in the Classics.

Johnston's parents came from two celebrated local families. His father is said to have been seventh from 'Stephanus Clericus', Stephen the Clerk, founder of the Johnston house in Aberdeenshire, and on his father's side the poet was also related to the aristocratic and powerful Hay family. Arthur Johnston's mother was Christian Forbes, daughter of William, seventh Lord Forbes, which meant the poet was related to various branches of that family. Arthur was one of thirteen children (six sons and seven daughters), several of whom achieved public distinction. His eldest brother, John, became sheriff of Aberdeen in 1630, while his youngest brother, William, held a chair of Latin and philosophy at the French Protestant University of Sedan, then later became Professor of Mathematics at Marischal College, Aberdeen.

The landscape Arthur Johnston knew as a child was both rural and grand. Caskieben lies close to the striking mountain Bennachie, which dominates the surrounding area. As a child, he was familiar with the streams of the Urie and Gadie, tributaries of the River Don which flow through the valley of the Garioch north of Bennachie. His poems suggest that Johnston was a keen fisherman, and mention several times these waters he knew from boyhood. While his childhood delights are seen through a nostalgic Classicising glow, Johnston grew up in a culture where it was still natural for educated young men to exalt through Classical parallels the rich farming landscape of Aberdeenshire with its fields, orchards, cattle, salmon and pearl-fishing, horse breeding and racing. So, for instance, he saw Kintore, where he went to school, as a place with a 'hippodromos' – a race-course – and it became linked in his mind with Elis in the Peloponnese, famous for its horse breeding and connected to the races of the Olympic games.

Though Kintore was some way off from Caskieben, efforts to set up a grammar school in Inverurie did not begin until 1606, and Kintore in Johnston's childhood was more important than Inverurie. In his poem 'Kintorium' (not included in the present book), he writes,

> Hic ego sum, memini, Musarum factus alumnus,
>   Et tiro didici verba Latina loqui.

> Here I remember being made the Muses' pupil,
> A wee boy learning to speak the Latin words.

From school in Kintore, Johnston progressed to university in Aberdeen. There he met his lifelong friend and fellow Aberdeen Latin poet David Wedderburn, who was born in 1580 and went on to become Rector of Aberdeen Grammar School as well as poet laureate of Aberdeen from 1620 – surely the first to hold such a post as a Scottish municipal poet. Wedderburn would eventually write six Latin elegies in Johnston's memory, calling Johnston 'poetarum sui seculi facile principis' (easily the leader among the poets of his age) and regarding him as a reborn Ovid. I suspect that

Johnston's fine poem 'In Obitum Iohannae Ionstonae' is written in memory of Wedderburn's first wife, Janet Johnstone, who married on 30 April 1611, gave birth to a son baptised on 25 March 1612, then died on 29 October 1613. Johnston's poem's intellectual movement from lamenting the premature death of a young bride to worrying about whether or not Johnston's own poetry will survive is somewhat disturbing, though not utterly untypical of poets. In another poem, written when he and Wedderburn were old men, Johnston recalled their youth together, climbing the Parnassus of Bennachie, and giving the local rivers Classical names in the sunlight of Apollo.

From Aberdeen, Johnston, like so many Scottish Latin poets of the Renaissance, headed to the continent. By 1599, aged about twenty, he was at the Casimirianum, or Casimir College of Heidelberg in Germany, where he matriculated on 11 September along with his fellow Aberdonian Walter Donaldson. Though the Casimirianum building burned down in 1693, the University of Heidelberg still occupies its site. Johnston was involved as a professor in a scholastic disputation there in 1601. Heidelberg was where Johnston would publish some of his earliest poems and, though the selection in the present volume concentrates on his shorter Scottish-related verse, he went on to write several long Latin poems relating to the political fortunes of the Palatinate. In 1603, when James VI of Scotland assumed the English throne, Johnston moved to the University of Sedan, invited there along with Walter Donaldson by the Prince of Sedan, the Duc de Bouillon. In 1604 he became Professor of Logic and Metaphysics in the university of this attractive walled and castellated city on the River Meuse. Six years later, when Walter Donaldson became Principal of the University of Sedan, Johnston was translated into Donaldson's old Chair of Physic. In June 1610 Johnston appears to have travelled to Padua to graduate as Doctor of Medicine; two of his continental poems are about the surgeon Julius Casserius (Casserio, 1545–1616) who taught medicine at Padua, gave anatomical demonstrations to students in the dissecting theatre, and after whom a ganglion is named.

At Sedan, Johnston became friends with another Scottish Latin poet, the former Glasgow and St Andrews professor and theologian Andrew Melville, who came to Sedan in 1611 as a refugee. Johnston seems to have relished the cosmopolitan make-up of the Sedan faculty. He wrote a series of poems as part of the 'Lusus Amoebaei', a friendly Latin exchange with the Silesian Daniel Tilen, a fellow author who later wrote against Scottish Presbyterians and Calvinist beliefs; Johnston's own son Daniel was baptised in Sedan in 1606. Around 1620 Johnston seems to have left Sedan, after becoming involved in a local row, and may have spent time in Paris, where some of his poetry was published. The great translator of Rabelais and over-the-top Scottish writer Sir Thomas Urquhart of Cromarty (c.1611–1660) later wrote in his *Jewel* that Johnston 'had been so sweetly imbued by the springs of Helicon that ... he was laureated poet at Paris and that most deservedly.'

It was during this period that Johnston wrote extended verse defences of Buchanan in a sort of learned flyting with his Scottish detractor Dr George Eglishem (whose surname seems to be connected with Eaglesham, near the modern East Kilbride). Accusing Eglishem of crimes against Apollo, Johnston portrays him as a quack doctor and quack poet, and deploys a rich knowledge of medical terminology and vituperation to do so. More nobly, Johnston also wrote substantial poems at the opening of the Thirty Years' War in 1619, pleading the case of Bohemia, where James VI's daughter Elizabeth was 'the Winter Queen' and which was attempting as a mainly Protestant state to throw off Austrian domination. It is likely that these poems helped Johnston win the approval of King James. He seems to have visited the London courts of James and of Charles I several times, and wrote a number of 'court poems' including those (included in the present selection) on the Queen's dances and on the Earl of Holland. Johnston's 1625 elegy for James VI and I laments not just the King's death but the fact that its occurrence meant the monarch was unable to help his daughter and the Bohemians in their struggle.

By this time, Johnston was back in Scotland, having returned by late 1622 to Aberdeen, bringing with him his first wife Marie de Cagniol (or 'Kynuncle' as an Aberdonian official wrote down her name). She died in 1624, the mother of Johnston's thirteen children, only six of whom survived. As well as Daniel, Marie's children included a daughter Francoise Johnston, baptised in Sedan in 1608. After his first wife's death, the poet married Barbara Johnston, who bore him further children (including a son who would become a Professor at King's College, Aberdeen), and who outlived her husband, dying in 1650. Johnston in Scotland was a man of substance and reputation. He seems to have been appointed *medicus regius* to King James in the early 1620s, and became a burgess of Aberdeen in 1622, taking quite a prominent part in local affairs. Just as he had been part of a network of poets in Sedan, so in Scotland Johnston enjoyed contact with poets and literary men. His circle included the learned Latin and English poet William Drummond of Hawthornden, who wrote in English (the principal language of Drummond's own verse) a letter to Johnston about the art of poetry. Johnston also knew many other leading Scottish cultural figures. One of these was Robert Baron whose scholarship in a formal scholastic Latin disputation had impressed listeners during King James's visit to St Andrews in 1617 when Baron was Professor of Philosophy there. By 1625 Baron was Professor of Divinity at Marischal College, Aberdeen, and one of a group of celebrated divines known as the 'Aberdeen Doctors', who would resist the National Covenant. Baron wrote theology in Latin and, though no Covenanter, did not disdain the writings of Calvin. Arthur Johnston addressed several poems to Baron, including one of his finest, the verse letter part of which is included in the present volume and in which Johnston writes of himself in rural Aberdeenshire in a style that draws on his master Ovid, exiled from Rome to the Black Sea outpost of Tomis. Complaining of ossifying in the boondocks and turning into a grotesque creature, Johnston presents his situation as worthy of the poet of the *Metamorphoses* and *Tristia*. However, it is clear from his acquaintance that Johnston was no solitary exile. His friends included Bishops Patrick and William Forbes and the successful trader William ('Willie the Merchant') Forbes of Craigievar who died in 1627 and for whom Johnston wrote the elegant obituary poem in this volume.

Readers of Johnston's poem for Forbes of Craigievar should realise that it pays tribute not to a plain, poor backwoods laird but to the man who had created in Craigievar Castle (now splendidly preserved as a National Trust for Scotland property) a particularly beautiful rural Aberdeenshire tower-house whose great hall has a stunning plaster ceiling emblazoned with coats of arms and complex geometrical patterns, while a huge plaster royal coat of arms is richly moulded above the great fireplace: Craigievar is a classic work of Scottish Renaissance art. It is characteristic of the highly sophisticated Johnston that another of his friends was George Jamesone, the humane Aberdonian portrait painter who, in the 1620s and 1630s, painted many portraits of Aberdeenshire nobility, including many of Johnston's subjects. Jamesone was called the 'Scottish Vandyke' by Horace Walpole, and has been described by Duncan Macmillan in his magisterial history of Scottish art as 'the first recognisably modern Scottish artist'. Jamesone knew William Drummond and his self-portrait shows him beside a large canvas whose subject looks like one from Classical mythology. This artist painted several 1620s oil portraits of the poet Johnston splendidly dressed with his pointed beard hanging over a white ruff; in one painting he holds a rose. In the poem addressed to his friend the painter and included in this volume Johnston writes elegantly about Lady Anne Campbell, Second Marchioness of Huntly, and his poem combines an enjoyment of the sort of conventions that may be found in the blazon of a Renaissance sonnet with a concluding injunction 'Fac similem tantum, qua potes arte, sui' (For if you aim to make a perfect picture/You only have to paint her as she is) which suggests a wish for a naturalistic style. George Jamesone painted the eighteen-year-old Anne Campbell in 1626 and that portrait still hangs at Gordon Castle in Aberdeenshire. It and Johnston's poem sit beautifully together.

In 1628 the Aberdeen printer Edward Raban published two Latin elegies by Johnston in a very slim volume (we know that William Drummond owned a copy), and in 1632 the same Edwardus Rabanus published two more substantial books of Johnston's own poetry, with his paraphrase of the Song of Solomon following in 1633. Raban published Johnston's paraphrase of the Psalms in 1637. In making these paraphrases Johnston had been encouraged by England's Archbishop Laud, eager no doubt to have Johnston produce a version to rival that of the Kirk's Buchanan. Where Buchanan had used many metrical variations according to the particular psalm he was paraphrasing, Johnston stuck to his customary hexameter and pentameter Ovidian couplet. His versions are surprisingly different from Buchanan's. While some Dutch readers were said to prefer Johnston to Buchanan, and on occasion Hebraists contended that Johnston was a more faithful translator, Buchanan's Psalms were generally held to excel those of Johnston, even if the latter are said to have 'a more quiet devotional air ... reminding one less of a heathen classic' as John Hill Burton put it in his account of *The Scot Abroad*.

All along, Johnston had been concerned to vindicate Buchanan's genius. Yet his own poems suggest not only admiration for Buchanan but also worry that the proximity of Buchanan's example may leave him too little room for his own work. In one of the poems in the present volume he sees Buchanan as second only to Virgil as a Latinist. Like several other Scottish Latin poets who succeeded Buchanan, however, Johnston was a resolutely and fluently Ovidian poet. His choice of Ovid as a model may have been in part temperamental, and in part a conscious attempt to do something different from Buchanan. Johnston has a more charming and gentle strain than Buchanan; his more moderate work is perhaps easier to love and is devoid of the presbyterian Reformation harshness that can give certain Buchanan poems extra bite. In his impressive poem on 'Joanna' (probably Janet) Johnston, Arthur Johnston moves from mourning a young woman to worrying ambitiously that his own gift may inevitably be overshadowed by that of the Scottish 'phoenix' Buchanan. Set out as a dialogue with his friend Wedderburn, this formal poem stages anxieties about Johnston's worth as a poet.

Johnston need not have worried. Relishing wordplay and learned references he has a quirky, playful intelligence that makes many of his best poems immediately appealing. His gifts also made him an astute anthologist and, with his friend William Drummond's brother-in-law, the senior judge and poet Sir John Scot whose tower-house of Scotstarvit near Cupar in Fife was an epicentre for Scottish Latin poetry, Johnston assembled the standard national anthology of Scottish Latin verse, the *Delights of the Illustrious Scottish Poets of this Age, Delitiae Poetarum Scotorum hujus aevi Illvstrivm*, published in Amsterdam by Johannes Blaeu in 1637 as part of a series of European national anthologies of Latin verse. In two volumes running to nearly thirteen hundred pages, this is a treasure-trove of Scottish poetry which remains largely forgotten. It is shameful that there is not a modern parallel text edition, and without it Scottish literary history has been badly misunderstood.

It is generally thought that Scot, whose library on the top storey of Scotstarvit Tower was emblematic of the Scottish Latin tradition, was the patron of this generous anthology, and Johnston the editor. Scot had studied at the University of St Andrews (where he endowed the Scotstarvit Chair of Humanity in 1620 and helped assemble a new class library for Latin teaching) and began the project of a major anthology of Scottish Latin poets in the 1620s. In a poem 'On the Bees Making Honey in the Temple of the Muses of Sir John Scot of Scotstarvit' the Scottish Latin poet John Leech (*fl.*1610–1624) writes of honey bees following their leader who

> Delegit certam sibi Scoti in culmine sedem,
>   Servat ubi vates bibliotheca sacros.

> Chose a place on Scot's tower's topmost storey
> Where his library holds sacred singers' songs.

It is likely that these were the volumes of poetry which Scot was collecting as he worked with Johnston on the project of the *Delitiae*. Leech's sense of Scotstarvit Tower as a place of honeyed cultural sweetness is reinforced by a statement quoted in Scot's 2004 *Oxford Dictionary of National Biography* entry that 'learned men came to him from all quarters, so that his house was a kind of college'. Though this statement may be exaggerated, there is no doubt that Scotstarvit Tower, like the nearby University of St Andrews, was a focus for the Scottish Latin tradition in poetry. The National Trust for Scotland which now cares for the fine and beautifully located Tower might consider making more of its status as a distinguished centre of Scottish Renaissance poetic and cultural life.

Scot and Johnston had been close for some time, and Johnston is thought to have been responsible for Scot's becoming a burgess of Aberdeen. Like

Johnston, Scot preferred Ovid to other Latin poets, and had a taste for elegy. Johnston pays Scot eloquent tribute in the dedication of the collection, and in verses within it, some of which are in this present book. Like other Scottish Latin poets, though even more so, Johnston likes to pun on the word 'Scot', which Classically-minded poets, conscious of writing far from the sunny Mediterranean, often associated with the Greek word 'skotos' (dark). So Johnston plays off the dour Scottish climate against the brilliance of his anthology's Latin stars. Curiously, for all their thirteen hundred pages, the two volumes of the small-format but finely printed *Delitiae* do not contain the poetry of Buchanan, whose relatively voluminous work may have been omitted because it was so readily available elsewhere, but the anthology does include many poets, one of whom is Johnston himself.

The year in which the *Delitiae* appeared, 1637, was also the year in which Johnston was elected Rector of the University and King's College of Aberdeen. This was a demanding post, both because of complex academic politics and because of the civil unrest in Scotland caused by religious and political warfare as King James's son, King Charles I, in London attempted to bring to heel the Scottish Kirk; his efforts were bitterly contested by the Covenanters. In 1641 on a visit to London, Johnston went to see his daughter who was married to an English clergyman in Oxford. He fell ill and died in that city. When in 1642 Sir John Scot of Scotstarvit sponsored an edition of Johnston's poems 'diligently revised by the author' and edited by the Reverend William Spang, continental minister of the Scots merchants' church at the port of Campvere, the dinky, small-format volume of over four hundred pages was published at Middelburg in Holland. European publication of this memorial collected poems was surely appropriate, given the pronounced European complexion of the Scottish Latin poets and of Johnston not least. Memorial verses by Johnston's old friend David Wedderburn link Johnston with the polylingual polymath the Admirable Crichton, with the admired Buchanan, and with Johnston's friend the Scottish refugee in Sedan, Andrew Melville, putting the situation pithily:

> Gallia Melvinum, Buchananum Scotia cepit,
>   Anglia Ionstonum, Mantua Crichtonium:
> Scilicet heroum claris decorare sepulchris
>   Orbem omnem laus est propria Scotigenum.

> France held Melville, Scotland held Buchanan,
>   England held Johnston, Mantua held Crichton:
> It seems the special glory of the Scots
>   To deck the whole wide world with heroes' graves.

As here, Johnston is always likely to be mentioned with Buchanan and with other Scottish Latin poets. Yet, as this book hopes to suggest, some of his finest poems which are among the works most likely to appeal to a modern audience are quite different from any of Buchanan's poems. The 'Encomia Urbium' or, to give them their fuller title, 'Celebriorum Aliquot Scotiae Urbium Encomia' (which has been translated as 'Epigrams in Honour of Some of the More Famous Cities and Towns of Scotland'), first appeared in the posthumous 1642 edition of Johnston's poems. The poet alluded to them in a short, undated poem sent to William Spang, probably quite late in Johnston's life. Sending to this Scot in Europe a gift of some of his Classical paeans to Scots towns, Johnston describes them as 'neither polished with the pumicestone nor decorated with Tyrian purple dye.' Yet if Johnston presents the poems as unpolished, the last line of his little poem hints at the fact that he nonetheless thinks they are likely to be appealing. If Spang likes them, Johnston writes, 'Non mea, sed patriae tu monumenta probas' (It's not *my* monuments you like, but Scotland's).

Perhaps these poems are likely to have a special appeal for Scottish readers, but that is not the limit of their attractiveness. The way in which Johnston melds local knowledge with learned Classical references is both deeply meant and tongue-in-cheek, so that it is sometimes difficult to tell how much he is hymning Scotland's towns, and how much he is expecting the reader to react with humour. Surely both elements are present. Only Arthur Johnston could have set Dundee beside the pyramids of Memphis, or asked 'Where are the pyramids of Inverurie?' Certainly Buchanan never wrote with such gentle humour, nor in his verse did he write in anything like this detail about the specifics of Scottish topography. The authentic details of his poems on such places as Brechin and Montrose might be set beside those of another project whose publication was sponsored by Sir John Scot of Scotstarvit, the 1654 publication by Blaeu in Amsterdam of the lovingly detailed maps of Scotland made by St Andrews-educated Timothy Pont (*c.*1565–1614). It was an age of the cartographical imagination, when location was celebrated in successive editions of the Englishman William Camden's immense Latin survey of the island *Britannia* from 1586 onwards. Yet the 'Encomia Urbium' are all the more attractive for being small-scale, while never pulling their punches.

The Classical model was the *Ordo Nobilium Urbium* of the fourth-century AD Latin writer Ausonius, a poet who, twelve centuries before George Buchanan, taught grammar and rhetoric in Bordeaux. Ausonius described twenty notable cities of the Roman world. Johnston confined himself to Scotland, and included two dozen settlements from Edinburgh to

Inverlochy, including Ayr, Cupar and Haddington, as well as larger cities. Though west-coast places feature, the concentration is on the east coast, especially the north-east. The Italian Renaissance scholar who called himself Julius Caesar Scaliger (and was father of the better known Calvinist Classicist J. J. Scaliger) wrote in the first half of the sixteenth century a series of 'Urbes' – city poems – and Arthur Johnston's Dutch friend Caspar Barlaeus similarly treated a group of Dutch towns. In Scottish literature, however, Johnston's group of poems, probably his last major work, seems to have been written in a spirit of competitive emulation of the poems which his fellow Aberdonian (and probable kinsman) John Johnston (c.1565–1611) had written on Scottish towns. A professor at St Andrews, John Johnston had seen his short poems about Edinburgh, Ayr, Glasgow, Stirling, St Andrews, Cupar, the East Neuk villages of Fife, Perth, Dundee, Montrose, Aberdeen and Inverness published in the 1607 edition of Camden's *Britannia*. Where John's poems are simply competent, however, Arthur's excel. Occasionally he follows John (as when both poets pun on the Latin 'Dei Donum' and the Scottish placename 'Dundee'), but in his own sequence of twenty-four poems Arthur Johnston makes much more of his opportunities. His poems are finer in quality as well as more daring in their claims.

This series of poetic landscapes has a unique place in Scottish verse which the passage of time has further burnished, so I have deliberately emphasised them by including a good number in this book. While I have chosen only some, I have placed them at the start of the selection of Johnston's poetry since, though written later in his life, they may form the most winning introduction to his work. The Johnston poems here are not arranged in chronological order of composition, which is often hard to calculate. A poem on Aberdeen has been added to my selection from the 'Encomia Urbium' group, and the poem on Inverurie from it has been held back until almost the end of the book. Several of these poems have been rightly admired, especially 'Andreapolis', the lovely poem about St Andrews which mixes lyricism, learning and humour. The 'Encomia Urbium' (which include rural as well as urban glimpses) may be seen as ancestors of the distinguished Scottish poetry of place and landscape that would be produced in the century following Johnston's death, most notably by the Classicist James Thomson whose work spurred the growth of the Romantic imagination. Arthur Johnston's topographical poems, however, are not Romantic. They are thoroughly Classical in a neo-Latin Scottish idiom. They sing.

* * *

While I started making the versions of Latin poems in this book simply because I wanted to make poems, another motive was wishing to include work by both poets in *The New Penguin Book of Scottish Verse* and in a further anthology of *Scottish Religious Poetry* which I co-edited in 2000. Having started, I came to like each poet in different ways, and felt both were wrongly forgotten. In making versions, I hoped to create some poems that would read as poems in English, whether or not they were word-for-word accurate. In any case, my Latin is so eroded that I could not make word-for-word accurate translations, even if I wanted to. I needed to use as 'cribs' several works gratefully singled out in the Acknowledgements section of this volume. Having published a few versions of Buchanan and Johnston in the *London Review of Books* and *Times Literary Supplement*, I was encouraged by some readers' comments (not least from Seamus Heaney) and by the opportunity to make a radio programme with Dave Batchelor about Buchanan for Radio 3 in 2005, when Tom Fleming proved a wonderful reader of the Buchanan poems. In the summer of 2005, the idea of this book took shape, and after that I tried to make more versions of work by both poets in order to show something of their range, even if this meant that sometimes my versions did not entirely content me as achieved poems in English. The result involves compromise, and I realise that some of the versions read better as English poems than do others. Also, some are fairly close renderings made with an eye on both earlier translations and on the original Latin, while others are definitely 'versions' and may be all the better for that. On occasion, to avoid the need for annotation I have built contextual information into my English versions. For readers who know Latin, and out of a wish to let the originals stand with their own dignity, I have presented this book in parallel text, even though there is not always a line-for-line equivalence – syntactical differences make this impossible to achieve between Latin and English. Since most readers are likely to read this book in English, I have put the English on the right-hand pages. I know I have been unable to do full justice to the range and complexity of either poet, and my selection of Johnston in particular has tended to concentrate on his shorter and Scottish-based poems. Nonetheless, five hundred years after the birth of George Buchanan and in an age which has generally forgotten about the Latin poets of Scotland, I hope this book will give readers some sense of what we've been missing.

R.C.,
The Poetry House,
University of St Andrews, 2006

GEORGE BUCHANAN

from Franciscanus

Campus erat late incultus, non floribus horti
Arrident, non messe agri, non frondibus arbos,
Vix sterilis siccis vestitur arena myricis,
Et pecorum rara in solis vestigia terris:
Vicini Deserta vocant. Ibi saxea subter
Antra tegunt nigras Vulcania semina cautes:
Sulphureis passim concepta incendia venis
Fumiferam volvunt nebulam, piceoque vapore
Semper anhelat humus: caecisque inclusa cavernis
Flamma furens, dum luctando penetrare sub auras
Conatur, totis passim spiracula campis
Findit, et ingenti tellurem pandit hiatu:
Teter odor tristisque habitus faciesque locorum.
Illic saepe animas torqueri Langius, illic
Saepe queri, et longas in fletum ducere voces
Audiit, aut voluit credi audivisse frequenter,
Et vitulabundos cacodaemonas, et per arenas
Caudarum longos sinuatim ducere tractus.
Saepe etiam infernae, quoties jejunus adibat
Antra, sibi visus nidorem haurire culinae.

His ubi jam vulgi stolidas rumoribus aures
Imbuerat, parat Exorcismum: circulus ingens
Ducitur, hunc intra spatio breviore minores.
In medio stabat palus, juxtaque catinus
Plenus aquae, sed cui cineremque salemque sacerdos
Addiderat multo cum murmure, nec sine anhelis
Flatibus. Hoc postquam scena est instructa paratu,
Langius ipse pater sacro venerandus amictu,
Circum omnem irrorat setosi aspergine sceptri,
Verbaque praecipiti contortuplicata rolatu
Convolvens, coelum ac terras adjurat et undas,
Et tremefacta imis Acherontia regna cavernis.

The Exorcist

A barren haugh. No flowers, no trees for miles.
No use for harvest. Barbed-wire thistles spatter
Dour, poisoned fields. Bare space. Hoofprints of cows.
Dysart, folk call it. Under desert earth
Vulcan's mile-long unmined coal still smeeks
In runnelled caves. Random, lung-clogging fires
Belch out all over through the veins of rock,
Firing up flumes of fumes, and, underfoot,
Pica-fine, pitch-black clouds smother the soil.
Jailed in dark caverns, sheer heat tries to burst
Up through drab, crusty, perforated ground
All over, fissuring that tired-out waste,
Reeking of sulphur. Father William Lang,
Franciscan spin doctor to James the Fifth,
Let on that he could hear lost souls being racked there,
Could tune in to their endless yells and yowls
And spot dark demons wildly trampolining,
Slewing their sinewy tails across the beach.
One day in Dysart on an empty stomach
He said he breathed the low cuisine of Hell.

So, after spinning this tremendous story,
Lang decks himself out as The Exorcist,
Scrawls an enormous circle inside which
Other much smaller circles are sketched out,
And drives a stake, dead-centre; plonks beside it
A crackling cauldron. Then, all mumbo jumbo
And last-gasp oaths, he stirs in salt and ashes.

Act Two. The Reverend Holy Father Lang,
Dressed to the nines, goes ladling holy water
All round, and, hocuspocussing like mad,
Denounces devils, then invokes the heavens,
Earth, firth, and all Acheron's bowel-dark kingdoms
Rifting and belching in the deepest depths.

Et jam nox aderat secreti conscia sacri,
Jamque e vicinis populus convenerat agris,
Matres atque viri, pueri innuptaeque puellae,
Scire avidi quo tanta cadant promissa: nisi ille
Conscia secreti formidans lumina et aures,
Esse procul magna jussisset voce profanos;
Quive sacerdoti non illa luce diserte
Cuncta susurrasset tacituram crimina in aurem:
Laica ne trepidi fugiant commercia manes,
Neve inhians praedae vel jejunus cacodaemon
Involet, et laceret sceleratorum unguibus artus.

Ducitur ad palum velut hostia rusticus ipse,
Ficta quidem gnarus cuncta, at formidine tanta
Attonitus, quam si Stygia egressurus ab alno
Aspiciat nudas mandentem Cerberon umbras;
Sive animo timor a puero conceptus, aniles
Fabellae haud modicus pueris plorantibus horror,
Sive locus fumo et caeca caligine opacus,
Et velut infernae terrebat imago culinae.
Caetera submoto clam cuncta peracta popello:
Sed tamen audiri gemitus, vocesque minantis
Daemonibus, mixtaeque preces, nulloque rogante
Interdum responsa dari: nunc tollere vultus
In coelum, nunc figere humi, nunc plangere pectus
Langius, et sacra templum conspergere lympha,
Donec avis lucis praenuntia spectra moneret
Cedere, et in veterem se denuo condere nidum.

Tum templo egressi, dicenda tacenda referre
Langius, umbrarum poenas, flammae rapidam vim
Lustralis: quot carnifices cacodaemones ollas
Admoveant, verubus quot figant, fluctibus umbras
Quot mersent gelidis, quot Missis cui levetur
Poena, velut civis Stygio vixisset Averno,
Ordine cuncta recensebat: neque credula deerat

Act Three. The Dark Night of The Sacred Secrets.
Hordes of local farmers crowd around:
Wives, husbands, nubile daughters come to gawp,
Itching to see what's up; but, just in case
They catch him out, Lang yells, 'Stand back! STAND BACK!
Especially you who have not made confession
Since yesterday, or else these trepidatious
Phantoms may flit before your uncleansed presence,
Or Cacodaemon with his greasy jowls
Gulp you right down and flense your sin-drenched shanks!'

Act Four. A local yokel, The Boy Martyr,
Is hauled out to the stake. He knows Lang's game,
But still he's shit-scared, just as if, about
To jump blithely ashore from Charon's ferry,
He catches slobbering Cerberus chomp up
The bodies of the damned. Maybe his granny's
Stories come back to haunt him, or it's just
That carbon copy of hell's kitchen-stink,
Dysart's midnight pitch-black darkness, spooks him.
The farmers cower. The exorcism goes on
With no one except Lang having a clue,
Though everybody hears groans, grumbles, voices
Threatening, then chanted prayers, answers
Flung out to questions nobody had asked.
One moment bowing to the dirt and beating
His chest, the next his eyeballs rolling round,
Lang goes for broke, and hoses holy water
All night, till the dawn chorus scares away
One last ghost way down to his ancient den.

Act Five. The folk go home. Lang cites as true
What no one really knows: the spirit's fate;
The bushfire heat of purgatorial flames;
How many pots and pans hell's demons stir;
How many souls they skewer on their spits;
How many souls get drowned in waves of ice;
How many masses it may take to let
Each soul off just a bit; it sounds as if
Lang wrote the Rough Guide to the Underworld.

Turba homini: purgatricis rediviva favillae
Gloria crescebat, multum indignante Luthero:
Et crevisset adhuc, nisi vel formidine captus,
Vel pretio victus, vel vino, rusticus ille
Anormis comes, Exorcismi proditor, eheu!
Cuncta revelasset taciti mendacia sacri.
Ex illo fluere, et retro sublapsa referri
Spes praedae, et nimium vivacis gloria veri
Crescere. Quapropter, moneo, dehinc fingite parce
Somnia, nocturnos lemures, miracula, ni fors
Aut apud extremos fieri dicantur Iberos,
Americosve, aut Aethiopas, calidove sub axe,
Et caput ignotis ubi Nilus condit arenis
Unde aderit nemo, qui testis dicta refutet.

Andreae Goveano

Alite non fausta genti dum rursus Iberae
    Restituis Musas, hic, Goveane, jaces.
Cura tui Musis fuerit si mutua, nulla
    Incolet Elysium clarior umbra nemus.

His audience loves it, and soon Purgatory's
Back in fashion, much to Martin Luther's
Disgust – and Purgatory's hoary glory
Would still be mushrooming, had it not been
For Lang's wee sidekick who, whether through fear,
Or for a bribe, or after one too many,
Spills all the beans – that Sorcerer's Apprentice,
That sad debunker of The Exorcist!
From then on all the hopes of Dysart shrivel.
Nothing can bar the Glory of the Truth.

So take heed after this not to make up
Fake phantoms, spooks that hoof it through the night,
Tales of the Unexplained, unless of course
They take place far from home, way out among
The Spaniards or the Coimbran Portuguese,
Or way, way out in Dark America,
Or underneath the Ethiopian sun,
Where no eye-witnesses can say you're wrong,
Or where the Nile's source hides out in the desert
And no one knows the Dysart Exorcist.

Inscription for the Tomb of the Portuguese Humanist André de Gouvea

Gouvea, you gave so much and got so little,
Bringing back Poetry to Portugal.
Your grave's here where, like Poetry, you struggled.
No soul's more splendid in the Elysian grove.

Ad Rectorem Scholae Conimbricae Mursam

O Domine Rector, Rex Scholae Conimbricae,
Miramur omnes hic tuam potentiam.
Beleago regni quantula est belua tui,
Ut nil sub ejus subditum non sit pedes?
Nil ille manibus non avaris inquinet?
Capros, et hircos, suculas, oves, boves,
Et universa pecora mactat, vendidat:
Volucresque coeli vendit, et pisces maris
Quicunque ponti semitas perambulant:
Pepones, cucumeres, pruna, porros, et nuces
Cosellianos quae per hortos germinant,
Coriandra, cepas, allium, nasturtium,
Samarcianos quae per hortos pullulant.
O Domine Rector, Rex Scholae Conimbricae,
Desideramus hic tuam prudentiam.

De Beleagone

... Et e macello philosophus prodit nouus,
Zenonis atsi prodeat de portico ...

In Beleagonem

... Nulla tuis dictis quod sit constantia, Maurus
    Indicium Lybici sanguinis esse putat.
Signa sui generis credit Judaeus acumen,
    Quodque tibi est lucri tam furiosus amor.

In Eundem

... Cuncta unde possit confici pecunia
Vendit, revendit, praestinat, habet quaestui.
Nec ullus opifex, emtor est, aut venditor,
Merx, ars, negotium, unde levis odor lucri
Spirat, quod ille non sagax praesentiat,
Non antevortat, occupetque et devoret:
Aut si id negatur, portiunculam tamen
Praerodat aliquam, solus et magnarius
Mercator, idem solus et scrutarius.
Si quis tot artes tractat unus sordidas,
Hoc axe natus, gente nec Judaeus est;
Beleago, dicam, has tractat artes sordidas ...

Beleago

Diogio de Murça, Head and King,
Rector of Coimbra University,
We all admire the way you've got ahead,
But your Sub-King Co-ordinator of
Commercialisation, your Head of Advanced, Enhanced
Entrepreneurship, that wee
Master Beleago, MBA
(Monster of Bestial Accumulation)
Whose ugly hooves tramp on our heads
Is so pigheadedly convinced
That he has wholly Mastered Being Ahead
Of us, your mere human resources, he
Goes and sells off everything: sells goats,
Sells pigs, sells cattle, killing
Whole herds so he can sell and sell;
Birds of the air, fish of the sea –
He sells the lot: your pears and nuts,
Plums, peppers, reconditioned cucumbers
Grown in your labs, your onions, garlic,
Capers and corianders sprouting
In students' grassy gardens – all for sale.
Dead magpies marketed as pheasants' breasts,
Goats' meat as mutton, broken bones jammed in your mince.
Lord Rector, Head of Coimbra's School,
Show us a better way to get ahead
Than that Belial-bellied Beleago,
Our no-brain, blackballed Baal of the Unbelles Lettres
Of Marketing, our Mall-mad Manager,
For what he says he possesses he doesn't possess,
What he says he professes he can't profess,
Iago-Beleago, Shylock of Market Stalls,
Server-up of venison sludged from pigs' balls,
Thrice winner of the Nobeleago Prize
For out-Cretaning Cretans with his Courses in Creative Lies,
Cretinous silly-git syllogist, philosobutcher, Zeno of Lard,
Exhibitionist, inquisitionist, circumcisionist,
Throatslitter, nestshitter, brainquitter, inkspitter, Grand
Inquisitor's Portuguese Libyajewish Supergrass who grassed

In Eundem

Nec foenerator alter illo doctior,
   Nec caupo quisquam argutior:
Mango nec ullus morbidos peritius
   Servos equosque adulterat:
Nec in macello ponderum minutias
   Sic lanius ullus exigit,
Lancem dolosam deprimitve cautius
   Fractis adaugens ossibus:
Seplasianae nec tabernae lucrio
   Interpolare astutior:
Nec publicanus e propinquis quispiam
   Ad omne lucrum acutior.
Et inter artes sordidas monopolium
   (Nam id laudo quod librarius)
Exercet, unus et veteramentarius,
   Et unus est scrutarius,
Negotiator unus est magnarius ...

Quas est professus se tenere, non tenet,
   Nec tractat artes, nec docet,
Nec scit docere, scire nec penitus studet.
   Sed olida convictoribus
Ut ponit hirci latera pro vervecibus,
   Corvosque pro caponibus,
Picasque caveae mortuas in carcere
   Pro phasianis suggerit:
Sic ille misero credit auditorio
   Se facile posse imponere;
Veterum Sophorum sic novis mendaciis
   Adulterare dogmata.
Cum syllogismi implicitus haeret retibus,
   Nutatque, sudatque, et stupet.
Dein ceu solutum sit probe impudentia,
   Quod peccat ignorantia,
Et ridet ipse, et caeteris est risui.
   Cur ergo quae nescit, docet?
Quae scit docere, non docet? mendacium,
   Quod prima ei sit artium ...

Me up, got me arrested, tested, tortured, chucked
In prison, that Magog of goats and groats,
That Papal brown-noser, that Sniffer-out-of-Heretics-in-his-own-Sandals,
That academic Vandal, I want to hear him caught and locked and trapped
In his own echoing 'Sell! sell! sell! sell! sell! sell!'
Forever, so I can sing
Your praises, Lord Rector, and pray
With a loud shout, a whoop, a from-the-heart 'Wey-hey-hey!' –
Baal-Iago, Beleago, BYE BYE!

This English version is a composite which draws on the several poems and extracts from Buchanan's 'Beleago' series printed opposite.

Ad Eundem Invictissimum Regem
De Hoc Commentario Georgius Buchananus

Cum tua sceptra Asiae gens Europaeque timeret,
    Et tremeret fasces terra Libyssa tuos:
Jamque jugi patiens Indus, nec turpe putaret
    A domino Ganges poscere jura Tago:
Inque tuis Phoebus regnis oriensque cadensque,
    Vix longum fesso conderet axe diem:
Et quaecunque vago se circumvolit Olympo,
    Luceret ratibus flamma ministra tuis:
Gaudebat tibi devictus, sibi redditus orbis,
    Nosse suos fines, justitiamque tuam.
Una aberat, oberatque tuis Mors saeva triumphis,
    Carpere victricem scilicet ausa manum.
Et comes huic tenebris nisa est Oblivio caecis
    Fortia magnanimum condere facta ducum.
Donec Apollineis se Tevius induit armis,
    Et spolia e victa Morte superba tulit:
Victurisque jubet chartis juvenescere vitae
    Prodiga pro patriae pectora laude suae:
Proque aevi paucis, quos Mors praeciderat, annis,
    Reddit ab aeterna posteritate decus.
Jure ergo invictus Rex es, quando omnia vincens
    Accessit titulis Mors quoque victa tuis.

A Commendation of the *Commentarius* of Diogio de Teive to King João III of Portugal

Omnipotens Portuguissimus,
Leolisbonus Rex, King Invictissimus,
Et Emperor Magnifikissikissimus,
Considering
How all Asian and European peoples
Fear your great sceptre,
How you are Lord of Libya's liberty,
How India is indisputably
Your slave, and Ganges ports are Portuguese,
And how Apollo, knowing your appellations,
Rises in the east, sets in the west,
Never once leaving lands that fear your name,
And how he struggles to complete his journey,
So big's your Empire, and how each small star
That circumvolves the trackless heavens shines
On your most royal imperial treasure ships –
Considering all this Portugalaxy
Of world-wide pride and fully-fêted feats,
No wonder the entire enormous globe,
Conquered by you and brought back to itself,
Rejoices in its limits and your justice.
Only one thing, the thing called rabid Death,
Threatened your trump-card. Death's cadaverous hand
Made a crude, rude attempt to grab your own
Imperial, victorious kingly fingers.
Oblivion, Death's familiar, tried hard too
To shroud heroic deeds in blackout dark,
Until your chronicler, Diogio Teive,
In his most noble *Commentarius*
About the Portuguese in India
(Printed in Coimbra, 1548),
Put on Apollo's armour and beat both
Death and Oblivion. In Teive's winning pages
He orders those brave hearts to live again
Who as staunch soldiers sacrificed themselves
For the pure honour of proud Portugal
And for your honour, King João, Emperor,

In Polyonymum

Lusitanicus unus es mare ultra et
Citra Algarbicus Indicusque Arabsque,
Persicus Guineusque et Africanus
Congusque et Manicongus et Zalophus;
Nec tuis titulis abest superbis
Aethiops nimio perustus aestu,
Nec circum triplicem refusus orbem
Cunctarum Oceanus parens aquarum;
Nec portus neque merx neque insula ulla est,
Lucelli unde levis refulget aura,
Quae te non titulo augeat. Tot ergo
Cui sunt nomina, nonne jure Regem
Multis nominibus vocabo magnum?
Sed Rex nominibus tot ille magnus,
Si belli furor aut mare aestuosum
Occludat piperariam tabernam,
Faenum fenore pransitabit emptum
Versuram faciet vel esuribit.

He gave them glory for all time to come
And gives you glory, João, unconquered King,
Making you Conqueror of All-Conquering Death.

To the Opposite of Anon

The north shore of the Mediterranean Sea
Calls you the King of Portugal, the south
Arch-Emperor of Goa, Allah's Vizier,
Sire Shah of Persia, Governor of Guinea,
Africa's Avatar, King of the Congo,
Mormaer-Boss of Bantu Mbanza Congo,
Mid-Mozambique's Magnificent Main Man –
Your titles take in mercilessly scorched
Ethiopian deserts and Poseidon's
Tripartite oceans. No port, trade, or isle
Glints with a hint of profit and escapes
Your wish to style yourself its sovereign owner,
Sir Shipshape Shop, Grand Duke Umpteenifer ...
So, while you stick more titles to your name,
I'll call you Great King Polyonymus,
But if war breaks out or tsunami strikes
Shut down your whole ridiculous peppershop,
Your name will be Earl Debt or Lord Starvation,
Skint, blasted King Imperium-Emporium ...

Brasilia

Africa deseritur, miles mendicat egenus,
  Vi sine tuta fugax oppida Maurus habet.
Accipit obscoenos Brasilia fusca colonos,
  Quique prius pueros foederat, arva fodit,
Qui sua militibus tollit, dat rura cinaedis,
  Jure sub adverso nil bene Marte gerit.

In Zoilum

Frustra ego te laudo, frustra me, Zoile, laedis:
  Nemo mihi credit, Zoile, nemo tibi.

Brazil

Africa's wasteland. Undernourished soldiers
Hold out their hands as Muslim cowards take
Morocco's towns. Now it's Brazil
Calls dirty colonists. Paedophile priests
Howk its dark earth, and that same King
Of Portugal who snatched Moroccan soil
Back from his own troops hands Brazil to bum-boys.
There is no justice in an unjust war.

Against Zoilus

I waste time praising you, Zoilus. You waste time dispraising me, too –
Because nobody believes me, Zoilus, and not a soul believes you.

Ad Peiridem Lenam

Lena tibi est genitrix, tu matris filia paelex,
    Et tua suscipiet filia matris onus.
Cumque tibi fratrem prudens natura negasset,
    In monachis fratrum tu quoque nomen amas.
Quam bene quod primis pater est tibi mortuus annis,
    Ne natae iam plus quam pater ille foret.
Exulat extremos tibi vir depulsus ad Indos,
    Proque viro lixas diligis atque coquos.
Consobrina suos tecum partitur amores,
    Et tibi crissanti est Aethiopissa tribas.
Nescio quid monstri celas, Leonora, reclusi,
    Quando tibi solum monstra pudenda placent.
Impietas odisse suos est maxima, verum
    Impietas sic est maior amare suos.

To a Bawd called Peiris

Yes, you're one true motherfucking daughter.
Your own girl's eager for her mother's job.
Nature was wise in giving you no brother,
Knowing you'd bed whole brotherhoods of monks.
Good thing your father died when you were young:
That saved him from your sheets. Your husband's gone
Far as he can to far-off India,
So in his place you shag wee greasy cooks
And sales reps. Other times your ladette cousin
Makes it a threesome and a big black dyke
Clambers on top to make you come and come.
Leonora, I don't know what perverts
You hide away: perverts are all you fancy.
The worst sin's to detest one's flesh and blood,
But your sin's worse: the way you love your own.

Ad Eandem [Leonoram]

Vive male, monachique tui lixaeque coquique,
  Mater edax, illex filia, nigra tribas.
Ne tamen interea vestri immemor arguar esse,
  Vos penes hoc nostri pignus amoris erit.

E Graeco Simonidis

Ut arma fugias, fata non fugies tamen.

Mair Leonora[*]

Wae wurth ye, wi yir monks, fleein merchants, cuiks,
Yir gutsy Maw, yir randie dochter, aye,
An yir black hing-tae! Jist in case, Leonora,
Ye think I'll ivver disremember ye,
Here's this wee luvesang aye tae mind me by.

From the Greek of Simonides

A man can flee from fighting, not from fate.

[*] Mair – *more*; wae wurth ye – *a curse on you*; fleein merchants – *sutlers*; gutsy – *voracious*; Maw – *mother*; hing-tae – *female lover*; disremember – *forget*; mind – *remember*.

Desiderium Lutetiae

O Formosa Amarylli, tuo jam septima bruma
Me procul aspectu, jam septima detinet aestas:
Sed neque septima bruma nivalibus horrida nimbis,
Septima nec rapidis candens fervoribus aestas
Extinxit vigiles nostro sub pectore curas.
Tu mihi mane novo carmen, dum roscida tondet
Arva pecus, medio tu carmen solis in aestu,
Et cum jam longas praeceps nox porrigit umbras:
Nec mihi quae tenebris condit nox omnia vultus
Est potis occultare tuos, te nocte sub atra
Alloquor, amplector, falsaque in imagine somni
Gaudia sollicitam palpant evanida mentem.
At cum somnus abit, curis cum luce renatis
Tecta miser fugio, tanquam mihi tecta doloris
Semina subjiciant, et solis moestus in agris,
Qua vagus error agit feror, et deserta querelis
Antra meis, silvasque et conscia saxa fatigo.
Sola meos planctus Echo miserata gementi
Adgemit, et quoties suspiria pectore duco,
Haec quoque vicino toties suspirat ab antro.
Saepe super celsae praerupta cacumina rupis
In mare prospiciens, spumantia coerula demens
Alloquor, et surdis jacto irrita vota procellis:
    O mare! quaeque maris vitreas, Nereides, undas
Finditis, in vestros placidae me admittite portus:
Aut hoc si nimium est, nec naufragus ire recuso,
Dummodo dilectas teneam vel naufragus oras.
O quoties dixi Zephyris properantibus illuc,
Felices pulchram visuri Amaryllida venti,
Sic neque Pyrene duris in cotibus alas
Atterat, et vestros non rumpant nubila cursus,
Dicite vesanos Amaryllidi Daphnidos ignes.
O quoties Euro levibus cum raderet alis.

Longing for Paris

Beautiful Amaryllis! I have missed you
For seven winters now and seven summers,
But neither seven lightning-struck Novembers
Nor seven long Junes broiling in the sun
Can stop my endless longing to be yours.
You are my morning song when cattle graze
The dewy grass, you are my song when noon
Scorches the landscape. When the gloaming throws
Long shadows everywhere, I sing of you.
Not even dark, obliterating midnight
Can hide your face from me. I say your name
And take you in my arms, love, as before.
All night ecstatic dreams destroy my sleep,
Then when sleep goes the light of day comes back,
Making me so mad I just must get out
Of all inhabited places, as if they
Had caused my craziness. I go away
Into the wilderness to be alone,
Wandering all over, tediously
Girning to caves and woods and listening rocks.
Only the sympathetic goddess Echo
Commiserates with me. Whenever I
Sigh she sighs back from nearby stony glens.
Time after time, high on vertiginous
Clifftop paths, gazing way out to sea,
I holler madly at blue, stormy waters
And yell my useless prayers to deaf gales.
   Ocean, with Nereids leaping from clear waves,
Carry me gently to the port I long for,
Or, if that's too much, since I'm already
Wrecked, I'm ready to risk any shipwreck
To see those shores I love. So many times
I've screamed into the West Wind howling there,
Those happy gales that blow towards Amaryllis,
Praying harsh Pyrenean crags won't ever
Stop those great sea winds, nor stormclouds slow them.
Tell Amaryllis I'm still mad about her.
So often when the East Wind's flitted by,

Aequora, dicebam, Felix Amaryllide visa,
Dic mihi, Num meminit nostri? Num mutua sentit
Vulnera? Num veteris vivunt vestigia flammae?
Ille ferox contra rauco cum murmure stridens
Avolat irato similis, mihi frigore pectus
Congelat, exanimes torpor gravis alligat artus.
Nec me pastorum recreant solamina, nec me
Fistula, Nympharumque leves per prata choreae,
Nec quae capripedes modulantur carmina Panes:
Una meos sic est praedata Amaryllis amores.
   Et me tympana docta ciere canora Lycisca,
Et me blanda Melaenis amavit, Iberides ambae,
Ambae florentes annis, opibusque superbae:
Et mihi dotales centum cum matribus agnos
Ipsi promisere patres, mihi munera matres
Spondebant clam multa: meum nec munera pectus,
Nec nivei movere suis cum matribus agni,
Nec quas blanditias tenerae dixere puellae,
Nec quas delicias tenerae fecere puellae.
Quantum ver hyemem, vietum puer integer aevi,
Ter viduam thalamis virgo matura parentem,
Quam superat Durium Rhodanus, quam Sequana Mundam,
Lenis Arar Sycorim, Ligeris formosus Iberum,
Francigenas inter Ligeris pulcherrimus amnes:
Tantum omnes vincit Nymphas Amaryllis Iberas.
Saepe suos vultus speculata Melaenis in unda
Composuit, pinxitque oculos, finxitque capillum,
Et voluit, simul et meruit formosa videri.
Saepe mihi dixit, Animi male perdite Daphni,
Cur tibi longinquos libet insanire furores?
Et quod ames dare nostra potest tibi terra, racemos
Collige purpureos, et spes ne concipe lentas.

I'll say, 'Sea squall, so happy to have seen
My happy Amaryllis, tell me now,
Does she still think of me? And is her hurt
Equal to mine? And does whatever's left
Of our old love still blaze up in her heart?'
The raging storm blasts by, blows itself out
Like an angry man, and leaves me out here, numb,
Chilled to the bone. Half-heartedly I try
To act the shepherd, tootling on a flute,
Dancing distractedly with country lassies.
The goat-hoofed songs of Pan are not for me.
I only want one lover, Amaryllis.
   Lycisca, dancing with sly castanets,
And bland Melaena – both made eyes at me –
Two Portuguese girls, lovely as young orchids,
Each rich, each self-assured. Their farmer fathers
Promised to give me as a wedding dowry
A hundred head of ewes, a hundred lambs,
To which their mothers promised to add more.
I was unmoved. Not all those snow-white lambs
And ewes, nor what those lovely girls would say,
Nor even what those lovely girls would do
Could win me over. Spring is always finer
Than winter, boyhood better than old age,
A girl outshines her three-times-widowed mother,
The Rhone excels Portugal's River Douro,
The Seine excels the Monda, and the Soane
The Sycoris, while that outstanding River
Loire, the loveliest of France's rivers,
Outshines the sinuous Spanish River Ebro –
In the same way, my love, my Amaryllis,
Is lovelier than all the Iberian girls.
Many times Melaenis puts on make-up
Squinting at her reflection in a pool,
Mascara-ing her eyes, shaping her hair,
Wanting to look as good as she can look.
Often she's said to me, 'My poor, lost Daphnis,
Why do you go on cuddling crazy dreams?
My land can give you everything you want.
Its juicy grapes are yours. Don't wait too long!'

Saepe choros festos me praetereunte, Lycisca
Cernere dissimulans, vultusque aversa canebat
Haec, pedibus terram, et manibus cava tympana pulsans:
Et Nemesis gravis ira, atque irritabile numen,
Et Nemesis laesos etiam punitur amores.
Vidi ego dum leporem venator captat, echinum
Spernere, post vanos redeuntem deinde labores,
Vespere nec retulisse domum leporem nec echinum.
Vidi ego qui mullum peteret piscator, et arctis
Retibus implicitam tincam sprevisset opimam,
Vespere nec retulisse domum mullum neque tincam.
Vidi ego qui calamos crescentes ordine risit
Pastor arundineos, dum torno rasile buxum
Frustra amat, (interea calamos quos riserat, alter
Pastor habet,) fragiles contentum inflare cicutas.
Sic solet immodicos Nemesis contundere fastus.
    Haec et plura Melaenis, et haec et plura Lycisca
Cantabant surdas frustra mihi semper ad aures.
Sed canis ante lupas, et taurus diliget ursas,
Et vulpem lepores, et amabit dama laenas,
Quam vel tympana docta ciere canora Lycisca
Mutabit nostros vel blanda Melaenis amores.
Et prius aequoribus pisces, et montibus umbrae,
Et volucres deerunt silvis, et murmura ventis,
Quam mihi discedent formosae Amaryllidos ignes:
Illa mihi rudibus succendit pectora flammis,
Finiet illa meos moriens morientis amores.

Frequently Lycisca, when I passed
Among the carnival, would turn her head
Away, pretending not to see, and stamp
The ground, and snap her castanets, then sing
Of angry Nemesis, that fiery spirit,
That Nemesis who punishes lost loves.
She'd sing, 'I've seen a hunter who would hunt
A hare look down his nose at a mere hedgehog
And end up losing hare and hedgehog both.
I've seen a fisherman, heart set on mullet,
Let every other fish slip through his net
As just not good enough: that man came home
With nothing at the end of the long day.
I've seen a shepherd regularly laughing
At his own reed bed, wanting only boxwood
To grow there so that he could make a lathe;
And while he laughed another harvested
The jilted reeds to make the perfect flute.
That's how too thrawn pride meets its Nemesis.'
   Wasting their time, Melaenis and Lycisca
Sang this and more, so I would hear their songs.
But dogs will lie with wolves, bulls mate with bears,
Hares pair with foxes, deer have sex with lions
Before Lycisca, all sly castanets,
And bland Melaena win me from my love.
The fish will leave the seas, the mountain ranges
Lose all their shadows, forests lose their birds
Before this searing love of Amaryllis
Leaves me. She was the French fire-raiser
Who scorched my heart. She set my soul alight.
We both will blaze with love until we die.

XXIII

Quid frustra rabidi me petitis, canes?
Livor, propositum cur premis improbum?
Sicut pastor ovem, me Dominus regit:
   Nil derit penitus mihi.
Per campi viridis mitia pabula,
Quae veris teneri pingit amoenitas,
Nunc pascor placide, nunc saturum latus
   Fessus molliter explico.
Purae rivus aquae leniter adstrepens
Membris restituit robora languidis,
Et blando recreat fomite spiritus
   Solis sub face torrida.
Saltus cum peteret mens vaga devios,
Errorum teneras illecebras sequens,
Retraxit miserans denuo me bonus
   Pastor iustitiae in viam.
Nec si per trepidas luctifica manu
Intentet tenebras mors mihi vulnera,
Formidem duce te pergere: me pedo
   Securum facies tuo.
Tu mensas epulis accumulas, merum
Tu plenis pateris sufficis, et caput
Unguento exhilaras: conficit aemulos,
   Dum spectant, dolor anxius.
Me numquam bonitas destituet tua,
Profususque bonis perpetuus favor;
Et non sollicitae longa domi tuae
   Vitae tempora transigam.

The Twenty-third Psalm
Paraphrased during Imprisonment
at the Hands of the Inquisition in Portugal

Rabid dogs, why waste your time on me?
Envy, why carry on with your corruption?
As a shepherd leads sheep, so the Lord leads me
And I shall want for nothing at his side.

One minute I feed quietly, the next
Lay my contented body calmly down
On lush Horatian pastures of green grass
Which tender lovely spring paints greener still.

Gentle gurgling water from a burn
Refreshes my tired limbs, encouraging
Inspiring breezes to revive me here
Under the scrutiny of the hot sun.

When my mind wandered, mad for trackless glens,
Seduced by tender, soft, erroneous words,
Then the good shepherd, sorry for my soul,
Led me at last back on to the right road.

Not even Death, in terrifying darkness,
Torturing me with his appalling hand,
Could make me fear to cleave to you, my leader;
Your shepherd's staff will stave off what I dread.

I see your tables set for the great banquet,
You pour your finest wine in brimming bowls,
You make my head shine with rich, soothing ointments,
And while they watch, my enemies feel fear.

Your goodness never will abandon me,
Nor will the favour showered on the good;
I will live out a long, untroubled life
Secure within the safe house of the Lord.

Adventus in Galliam

Jejuna miserae tesqua Lusitaniae,
Glebaeque tantum fertiles penuriae,
Valete longum. At tu beata Gallia
Salve, bonarum blanda nutrix artium,
Coelo salubri, fertili frugum solo,
Umbrosa colles pampini molli coma,
Pecorosa saltus, rigua valles fontibus,
Prati virentis picta campos floribus,
Velifera longis amnium decursibus,
Piscosa stagnis, rivulis, lacubus, mari;
Et hinc et illinc portuoso littore
Orbem receptans hospitem, atque orbi tuas
Opes vicissim non avara impertiens;
Amoena villis, tuta muris, turribus
Superba, tectis lauta, cultu splendida,
Victu modesta, moribus non aspera,
Sermone comis, patria gentium omnium
Communis, animi fida, pace florida,
Jucunda, facilis, Marte terrifico minax,
Invicta, rebus non secundis insolens,
Nec sorte dubia fracta, cultrix numinis
Sincera, ritum in exterum non degener:
Nescit calores lenis aestas torridos,
Frangit rigores bruma flammis asperos,
Non pestilentis pallet Austri spiritu
Autumnus aequis temperatus flatibus,
Non ver solutis amnium repagulis
Inundat agros, et labores eluit.
Ni patrio te amore diligam, et colam
Dum vivo, rursus non recuso visere
Jejuna miserae tesqua Lusitaniae,
Glebasque tantum fertiles penuriae.

Coming to France

Badlands of Portugal, bye-bye
Forever, starving crofts whose year-round crop
Is lack of cash. And you, fair France, bonjour!
Bonjour, adoring sponsor of the arts,
Your air's to die for, and your earth's so rich
Vineyards embrace your warm, umbrageous hills,
Cows crowd your pastures, glens gabble with burns,
Broad, open meadows fan out fields of flowers;
Sailboats go gliding down long waterways,
Fish throng your ponds, lochs, rivers, and the sea
Where, left and right, your harbours greet the world
With open arms. Unstinting, smiling France,
Your towns are stunners, safe, walled, turreted,
Sights for sore eyes, stacked out with shining roofs;
Your folk are never pushy, but plain-speaking,
Well-dressed, well-fed, so ready to be friends.
France, *alma mater* of the universe,
Faithful, happy, flourishing at peace,
Jocund and easy, but grim-faced in war,
Unbeatable, but not flushed with success.
When the going's tough you show true grit. You stand,
Defender of the true faith, with no time
For foreign bigots' fads. Well-balanced France,
Your summer's free from arid heat. Your winter
Gives up its bleak excesses at your hearth.
No east wind plagues make autumn faces pale,
No spring floods drown your farms with fast-thawed ice.
France, if for just one instant in my life
I cease to love you as my *patria*,
Send me straight back to Portugal's dour badlands,
Those crofts whose only crop is lack of cash.

De Equo Elogium

Caetera rerum opifex animalia finxit ad usus
Quaeque suos, equus ad cunctos se accommodat unus:
Plaustra trahit, fert clitellas, fert esseda, terram
Vomere proscindit, dominum fert, sive natatu
Flumina, seu fossam saltu, seu vincere cursu
Est salebras opus, aut canibus circundare saltus,
Aut molles glomerare gradus, aut flectere gyros,
Libera seu vacuis ludat lascivia campis.
Quod si bella vocent tremulos vigor acer in artus
It, domino et socias vomit ore et naribus iras,
Vulneribusque offert generosum pectus, et una
Gaudia, moerores sumit ponitque vicissim
Cum domino. Sortem sic officiosus in omnem,
Ut veteres nobis tam certo foedere iunctum
Crediderint mixta coalescere posse figura,
Inque Pelethroniis Centauros edere silvis.

Jacobo Sylvio

Sylvius hic situs est, gratis qui nil dedit unquam:
   Mortuus et, gratis quod legis ista, dolet.

Horse Hymn

God manufactured every other beast
For just one job. Only the horse
Does everything. He hauls great wagons,
Lugs pack-saddles, draws chariots, ploughs fields,
Carries his master, swimming river-crossings,
Leaping each ditch, traversing stony ground,
Coursing round woods with hounds, slow-trotting, wildly
Galloping back, or cantering for fun
On open grassland. Then, if war demands,
Vigour kicks in, nervous excitement builds
Till horse and master snort together, angry,
Charging into battle, sharing highs
And disappointments, finding, losing each.
The horse is so loyal that the Ancients dreamed
He could be one with humans, could just fuse
Into a mixed horse-man, man-horse – hybrid
Centaurs in the Pelethronian woods.

On James Wood

Here's James Wood's grave. Each gift he gave
He made the recipient pay.
Even in his coffin he's sorry
You're reading this gratis today.

De Nicotiana Falso Nomine Medicaea Appellata

Doctus ab Hesperiis rediens Nicotius oris
  Nicotianam rettulit,
Nempe salutiferam cunctis languoribus herbam,
  Prodesse cupidus patriae.
At Medice Catharina, KHATHARMA luesque suorum,
  Medea saeculi sui,
Ambitione ardens, Medicaeae nomine plantam
  Nicotianam adulterat;
Utque bonis cives prius exuit, exuere herbae
  Honore vult Nicotium.
At vos auxilium membris qui quaeritis aegris,
  Abominandi nominis
A planta cohibete manus, os claudite, et aures
  A peste taetra occludite;
Nectar enim virus fiet, panacea venenum,
  Medicaea si vocabitur.

Can Damage Your Health

When clever Nicot, MD, ChB,
Sailed back with baccy from Virginia's coast,
Cleverly he called it Nicotine,
A totally breath-taking panacea –
And really thought he'd done his country good;
But that Medea of the foul Medicis,
Coughed up by fouled Florence, cancerous Catherine
(Aka Cath, Catharsis of Catarrh),
Wanting to make a worse name for herself,
Rechristened nicotine the 'herbe médicée',
And so, puffed up with her Medici Herb,
After she'd pillaged her own citizens
She wanted next to nick his plant from Nicot.
Now, you who really feel under the weather,
Lay off that weed with an unlucky name.
Shove in your earplugs. Nil by mouth. It's deadly.
Even the best stuff from the cleverest medic
Will kill you when called after a Medici.

Jacobo IV. Regi Scotorum

Fama orbem replet, mortem fors occulit: at tu
   Desine scrutari quod tegat ossa solum.
Si mihi dent animo non impar fata sepulchrum,
   Angusta est tumulo terra Britanna meo.

Maria Regina Scotiae Puella

Ut Mariam finxit natura, ars pinxit: utrumque
   Rarum et solertis summum opus artificis.
Ipsa animum sibi dum pingit, sic vicit utrumque,
   Ut natura rudis, ars videatur iners.

To James IV, King of Scots

I fell at Flodden, and my corpse is lost.
Leave it. The whole earth knows
If fate could find a place to fit my spirit,
Britain would be too small to be my tomb.

The Young Girl Mary, Queen of Scots

In Mary shine both nature's work and art's.
Nature so formed her that high art is apt.
Yet both are outshone by her heart and mind
So nature seems crude and high art inept.

Francisci Valesi et Mariae Stuartae, Regum Franciae et Scotiae, Epithalamium

a
Unde repentino fremuerunt viscera motu?
Cur Phoebum desueta pati praecordia anhelus
Fervor agit, mutaeque diu Parnassidos umbrae
Turba iterum arcanis renovat Paeana sub antris?
Nuper enim, memini squalebat marcida laurus,
Muta chelys, tristis Phoebus, citharaeque repertor
Arcas, et ad surdas fundebam vota sorores.
Nunc Phoebi delubra patent, nunc Delphica rupes
Panditur, et sacro cortina remugit ab antro.
Nunc lauro meliore comas innexa sororum
Turba venit, nunc Aoniae non invida lymphae
Irrigat aeternos Pimplei ruris honores,
Laetaque Pieriae revirescit gloria silvae.
Fallimur? An nitidae tibi se, Francisce, Camoenae
Exornant? Tibi serta parant, tibi flore recenti
Templa novant? Mutumque diu formidine Martis
Gaudent insolitis celebrare Helicona choreis?
Scilicet haud alius nemoris decerpere fructus
Dignior Aonii, seu quem numerare triumphos
Forte juvat patrios, seu consecrata Camoenis
Otia: sic certe est. Hinc laeto compita plausu
Cuncta fremunt: legumque exuta licentia frenos
Ludit: Hymen, Hymenaeus adest: lux illa pudicis
Exoptata diu votis, lux aurea venit:
Venit. Habes tandem toties quod mente petisti,
O decus Hectoridum juvenis: jam pone querelas,
Desine spes nimium lentas, jam desine longas
Incusare moras, dum tardum signifer annum
Torqueat, ignavos peragat dum Cynthia menses.
Grande morae pretium fers: quod si prisca tulissent
Secula, non raptos flesset Menelaus amores,

Epithalamium
for Francis of Valois and Mary Stuart,
Monarchs of France and Scotland

a
Where does the birth-pang of a poem start?
Why do I feel the hot breath of Apollo
Fire up this heart that's gone so long unstirred?
How come from dark, remotest glens and cols
Of Ben Parnassus now the Muses dance
Towards me again, chanting a hymn of praise?
Moments ago, the poet's laurel was withered,
The lyre was mute, Apollo in the dumps,
As moody as the cithara's inventor,
Arcas; when I invoked those Sisters Muse
They turned a rubber ear. I lost all hope.
But now Apollo throws his shrine's doors wide,
Delphi's in action and the sacred sisters
Leap with fresh laurels from its glorious cave.
Ausonian waters splash the countryside,
Pierian forests are ablaze with green.
Some mistake surely? Francis, is it true
The Muses wear their garlands just for you?
Deck themselves out and strew the holy shrines
With flowers for you alone? Where Helicon
So long lay silent and in awe of Mars
All's song and dance. Prince Francis, true enough
No one more deserves the Aonian fruits,
Either in terms of great ancestral triumphs
Or hours devoted to the Muses' work.
Today's a day the streets are full of cheering,
A day for letting go, whooping it up
With Hymen, Hymenaeus, here with us.
A golden dawn, devoutly prayed for, dawns.
So, Prince, Hector's descendant, now at last
You'll possess what you've longed for. Don't grump, then,
About deferred desires and long, long waits,
The year's slow round when drab months last forever.
Your patience wins a prize which, had the ancients
Won it, would have meant that Menelaus

Et sine vi, sine caede Phrygum Cytherea probatae
Solvere Priamidae potuisset praemia formae.
Digna quidem facies, quam vel trans aequoris aestus
Classe Paris rapiat, vel conjurata reposcat
Graecia: nec minus est animi tibi, nec minor ardor
Quam Phrygio Grajove duci, si postulet arma
Conjugii tutela tui. Sed mitior in te
Et Venus, et teneri fuit indulgentia nati,
Qui quod ames tribuere domi: puerilibus annis
Coeptus amor tecum crevit: quantumque juventae
Viribus accessit, tanto se flamma per artus
Acrius insinuans tenerum pascebat amorem.
Non tibi cura fuit, quae saepius anxia Regum
Pectora sollicitat, longinquae obnoxia flammae:
Nec metus is torsit, veri praenuntia fama
Ne vero majora ferat, dum secula prisca
Elevat, et primum formae tibi spondet honorem:
Cera nec in varias docilis transire figuras
Suspendit trepidam dubia formidine mentem:
Nec tua commisti tacitis suspiria chartis,
Rumorisque vagam timuisti pallidus umbram.
Ipse tibi explorator eras, formaeque probator,
Et morum testis. Nec conciliavit amorem
Hunc tibi luxuries legum indignata teneri
Imperio, aut primis temerarius ardor ab annis:
Sed sexu virtus, annis prudentia major,
Et decori pudor, et conjuncta modestia sceptris,
Atque haec cuncta ligans arcano gratia nexu.
Spes igitur dubiae, lentaeque facessite curae,
Ipse tuis oculis tua vota tuere, probasque:
Speratosque leges sine sollicitudine fructus,
Nullaque fallacis delusus imagine somni
Irrita mendaci facies convicia nocti.
Exspectatus Hymen jam junget foedere dextras,
Mox etiam amplecti, mox et geminare licebit
Basia, mox etiam non tantum basia: sed tu,
Quamlibet approperes, animo moderare: beatum
Nobiscum partire diem, tu gaudia noctis
Solus tota feres: quanquam neque gaudia noctis
Solus tota feres: et nos communiter aequum est

Never would have wept for kidnapped Helen
Whose beauty Paris knew he had to filch
Across the surging sea; whose beauty Greeks
Joined forces to win back. Yet in your case
Pale Venus would have given Priam's son
The lovely Helen with no need for war.
Francis, you're brave as any Greek or Trojan,
And you would fight to keep your young wife safe,
But Venus smiled on you, and so did Cupid,
In giving you a princess close to home.
From infancy, you grew up loving her.
The flame of longing made you a strong boy
And nourished the deep tenderness of passion.
Unlike so many kings, you did not need
To worry about wooing from afar,
Nor fear reporters, garbling the plain truth,
Might hype it up. Reporters pay scant heed
To classic beauties from antiquity
But celebrate the models of today.
Francis, you haven't had to sigh by letter,
Pale and unsure, afraid of every rumour.
You saw her for yourself, saw she was lovely.
You knew her good. Your love was not some crush
That crassly misbehaves, nor a teenage fad,
But you knew she was better than all women,
Wiser than youth, and decorously lovely,
Modest yet royal, with an inner grace
Joining her virtues in a secret bond.
Away with nagging doubts and doubtful hopes!
You see right here the answer to your prayers;
Without anxiety you pluck the fruits
You longed for. You'll not toss in bed at night
Fruitlessly girning that some dream-girl's tricked you.
Now Hymen, whose arrival you've awaited,
Will come at last to join your hands in marriage.
Time soon to hug and kiss and more than that –
Do what you want at night – but keep this day
To share with us in communal good fun.
You'll have the night's delights all to yourselves,

Laetitiam gaudere tuam: communia vota
Fecimus, et sacras pariter placavimus aras,
Miscuimusque preces, et spesque metusque tuosque
Sensimus affectus: aegre tecum hausimus una
Taedia longa morae. Superi nunc plena secundi
Gaudia cum referant, sensus pervenit ad omnes
Laetitiae, mentemque ciens renovata voluptas
Crescit, et exsultant trepidis praecordia fibris.
Qualis ubi Eois Phoebus caput extulit undis
Purus, et auratum non turbidus extulit axem,
Cuspide jucundae lucis percussa renident
Arva, micat tremulo crispatus lumine pontus,
Lenibus aspirat flabris innubilis aer,
Blanda serenati ridet clementia coeli:
At si nubiferos effuderit Aeolus Austros,
Et pluviis gravidam coelo subtexuit umbram,
Moesta horret rerum facies, deformia lugent
Arva, tument fluctus, campis gravis incubat aer,
Torpet et obductum picea caligine coelum:
Sic ex te populus suspensus, gaudia, curas,
Moeroresque trahit: rosea nec sola juventa
Florida, nec spatiis quae te propioribus aetas
Insequitur, genio indulgent, vultuque soluto
Lusibus exhilarant aptos juvenilibus annos;
Hunc posita vultus gravitate severior aetas
Laetatur celebrare diem, matresque verendae
Non tacito hunc, tacitoque optat virguncula voto.

b
Quid loquar humanas admittere gaudia mentes?
Ipsa parens rerum totos renovata per artus
Gestit, et in vestros penitus conspirat honores.
Aspice jam primum radiati luminis orbem
Semper inexhausta lustrantem lampade terras,
Ut niteat, blanda ut flagrantes mitiget ignes
Temperie, ut cupidos spectacula vestra tueri
Purpureo vultus maturior exserat ortu,
Serius occiduas currus demittat in undas,
Ut gelidos repetens flamma propiore triones
Contrahat aestivas angusta luce tenebras.

But it is right we too should taste your joy.
We too have wished, we too have sacrificed
At the same altars, mixed our prayers with yours,
Felt in our hearts your hopes, fears, and affections.
Like you we've waited long and nervously
And, now the good gods give us back delight,
We mark with you a universal gladness
That grows and grows to quicken all our hearts.
As when Apollo blazes from the waters
Of the Indian Ocean in a flawless dawn,
And fields, and endless sparkling waves, and pure
Breezily azure skies reflect his light,
But if the god of winds blasts from the south,
Blowing up a monsoon between earth and heaven,
The whole globe shudders, deluged fields go grey
And grim, floodwaters rise, and clouds weigh down
The whole clogged sky with pitch-black foggy mirk –
Just so your kingdom's people take their cue
For joy or sadnesss from the way you act.
Your young pals party wildly and play hard
As youth does everywhere, your elders too
Chuck aside their hard-earned *gravitas*
And gladly celebrate this happy day
Old grandmothers have prayed for with strong voices,
And pure young girls have prayed for, lips shut tight.

b
Say it again: today's a holiday.
Nature herself frisks with us, young once more,
Showering you with fresh honours. See the sun
Lighting the wide world with its endless light,
Shading its blaze to gaze on your great day
With gentle mildness, till at early dusk
It drowns its chariot in the sea out west,
Or, trying to melt the Arctic, grazes earth,
Shortening summer's darkness with one skelf
Of tapering light. All earth renews itself

Ipsa etiam tellus virides renovatur amictus,
Et modo pampineas meditatur collibus umbras,
Et modo messe agros, modo pingit floribus hortos:
Horrida nec tenero cessant mansuescere foetu
Tesqua, nec armati spina sua brachia vepres,
Nec curvare feros pomis aviaria ramos:
Inque omnes frugum facies bona copia cornu
Solvit, et omniferum beat indulgentior annum,
Pignoris hoc spondens felices omine taedas.

C
Fortunati ambo, et felici tempore nati,
Et thalamis juncti! Vestram concordia mundi
Spem fovet, aspirat votis, indulget honori:
Atque utinam nullis unquam labefacta querelis
Conjugium hoc canos concordia servet in annos.
Et (mihi ni vano fallax praecordia Phoebus
Impulit augurio) quem jungit sanguinis ortus,
Et commune genus proavum, serieque perenni
Foedus amicitiae solidum, quem more vetusto
Sancta verendarum committunt foedera legum,
Nulla dies unquam vestrum divellet amorem.
Vos quoque felici lucent quibus omine taedae,
Quo studium, populique favor, quo publica regni
Vota precesque vocant, alacres accedite: tuque
Tu prior O Reges non ementite parentes,
Hectoride juvenis, tota complectere mente
Quam dedit uxorem tibi lex, natura sororem,
Parentem imperio sexus, dominamque voluntas,
Quam sociam vitae tibi conjunxere parentes,
Et genus, et virtus, et forma, et nubilis aetas,
Et promissa fides, et qui tot vincula nectens
Firmius arctat amor totidem per vincula nexus.
Si tibi communi assensu connubia Divae
Annuerent, Paris umbrosa quas vidit in Ida,
Permittantque tuo socias tibi jungere taedas
Arbitrio, quid jam, voti licet improbus, optes
Amplius? Eximiae delectat gratia formae?
Aspice quantus honos frontis, quae gratia blandis
Interfusa genis, quam mitis flamma decoris

Grass-green again, and watches vineyards swathe
Hillsides, sees fields dappled with crops, and gardens
Restocked with flowers, and even wildernesses
Tamed with fresh berries from sharp, straggly brambles,
Trees burdened under apple crops and birdsong,
A cornucopia of richest fruits
Blessing this year in which all life grows rich,
All heralding your promised happy marriage.

C
A happy couple, born in well-blessed times,
And twined in marriage. Global harmony
Fosters your hope, your wishes, and your pride,
And how I hope this union will last long
Till you are old and grey, carefree and glad,
And, if Apollo grants me second sight,
I say with confidence no day will dawn
When fate will stop a love which ancestry
And royal generations have contracted,
Which ancient pacts of friendship have renewed
And lawful ceremony sealed with justice.
Go, then, and blaze the way with wedding torches
And laughter linking all your peoples' hopes,
Prayers, good wishes. Francis, you go first,
Sure in royal birth, a Prince of Hector's line,
Clinch in your heart your lawful wedded wife,
Your natural co-equal whom her sex
Gives you as one obedient to your wish,
Whose own free choice has made her now your spouse,
Whose parents' gift makes her your life's companion,
Whom kinship, virtue, and nobility,
Loyalty, vows, and love all bind to you.
And if those goddesses whom Paris saw
Once in Mount Ida's shade smile on your nuptials,
Letting you choose a love-match, then what more
In all this whole wide world might you now ask?
Beauty's finesse, high forehead, dimpled cheek,
The gentle light that's laughing in her eyes –

Fulguret ex oculis, quam conspirarit amico
Foedere cum tenera gravitas matura juventa,
Lenis et augusta cum majestate venustas.
Pectora nec formae cedunt exercita curis
Palladiis, et Pierias exculta per artes
Tranquillant placidos Sophia sub praeside mores.

d
Si series generis longusque propaginis ordo
Quaeritur: haec una centum de stirpe nepotes
Sceptriferos numerare potest, haec regia sola est,
Quae bis dena suis includat secula fastis;
Unica vicinis toties pulsata procellis,
Externi immunis domini: quodcunque vetustum
Gentibus in reliquis vel narrat fama, vel audet
Fabula, longaevis vel credunt secula fastis,
Huc compone, novum est. Ampla si dote moveris,
Accipe dotales Mavortia pectora Scotos.
Nec tibi frugiferae memorabo hic jugera glebae,
Aut saltus pecore, aut foecundas piscibus undas,
Aut aeris gravidos et plumbi pondere sulcos,
Et nitidos auro montes, ferroque rigentes,
Deque metalliferis manantia flumina venis,
Quaeque beant alias communia commoda gentes.
Haec vulgus miretur iners, quique omnia spernunt
Praeter opes, quibus assidue sitis acris habendi –
Tabifico oblimat praecordia crassa veneno.
Illa pharetratis est propria gloria Scotis,
Cingere venatu saltus, superare natando
Flumina, ferre famem, contemnere frigora et aestus;
Nec fossa et muris patriam, sed Marte tueri,
Et spreta incolumem vita defendere famam;
Polliciti servare fidem, sanctumque vereri
Numen amicitiae, mores, non munus amare.
Artibus his, totum fremerent cum bella per orbem,
Nullaque non leges tellus mutaret avitas
Externo subjecta jugo, gens una vetustis
Sedibus antiqua sub libertate resedit.
Substitit hic Gothi furor, hic gravis impetus haesit
Saxonis, hic Cimber superato Saxone, et acri

All show she fuses wisdom with her youth,
Effortlessly majestic, subtly lovely.
Nor does her cleverness, preoccupied
With all Athene's work, yield to her beauty,
But, educated by the nimble Muses,
Her wisdom nourishes profound content.

d
Genealogical research has proved
She is descended from a hundred royals.
Only she has a lineage which holds
Two thousand years of monarchs' marriages,
Her people much attacked by hostile neighbours
Yet always free of foreign domination.
Whatever folktales say of ancient races,
Trust true research: compare things with today.
If what you long for is a generous dowry
Then Scottish fighting spirit is just that.
No need for me to list or catalogue
The many fertile acres, pastures, firths
Brimful of fish, the lead and copper mines,
Mountains that glint with gold or bulge with iron,
Burns flowing from rich veins of minerals.
Commodities like these commonly gladden
Foreigners, and are gawped at by the raw
Materialist mob who want hard cash
And do not care for the environment,
But the Scots' glory is to hunt and fish,
Swimming deep rivers, braving hunger, friend
To heat and cold alike, not looking after
Their native heath with trenches and high ramparts
But fighting for its honour with their lives.
They keep their word. They cherish loyal frienship.
They value character and not career.
So when war ravaged all the world, and nowhere
Maintained its constitution in the face
Of Roman rule, one ancient people prized
In Scotland here unbeaten independence.
Here Pictish fury did not cross the line,
Invading Saxons and then Danes were smashed,

Perdomito Neuster Cimbro. Si volvere priscos
Non piget annales, hic et victoria fixit
Praecipitem Romana gradum: quem non gravis Auster
Reppulit, incultis non squalens Parthia campis,
Non aestu Meroe, non frigore Rhenus et Albis
Tardavit, Latium remorata est Scotia cursum:
Solaque gens mundi est, cum qua non culmine montis,
Non rapidi ripis amnis, non objice silvae,
Non vasti spatiis campi Romana potestas,
Sed muris fossaque sui confinia regni
Munivit: gentesque alias cum pelleret armis
Sedibus, aut victas vilem servaret in usum
Servitii, hic contenta suos defendere fines
Roma securigeris praetendit moenia Scotis:
Hic spe progressus posita, Carronis ad undam
Terminus Ausonii signat divortia regni.
Neve putes duri studiis assueta Gradivi
Pectora mansuetas non emollescere ad artes,
Haec quoque, cum Latium quateret Mars barbarus orbem,
Sola prope expulsis fuit hospita terra Camoenis.
Hinc Sophiae Grajae, Sophiae decreta Latinae,
Doctoresque rudis formatoresque juventae
Carolus ad Celtas traduxit: Carolus idem
Qui Francis Latios fasces, trabeamque Quirini
Ferre dedit Francis, conjunxit foedere Scotos:
Foedere, quod neque Mars ferro, nec turbida possit
Solvere seditio, aut dominandi insana cupido,
Nec series aevi, nec vis ulla altera, praeter
Sanctius et vinclis foedus propioribus arctans.
Tu licet ex illa numeres aetate triumphos,
Et conjuratum cunctis e partibus orbem
Nominis ad Franci exitium, sine milite Scoto
Nulla unquam Francis fulsit victoria castris,
Nulla unquam Hectoridas sine Scoto sanguine clades
Saevior oppressit: tulit haec communiter omnes

Then, next, after the Danes, a Norman horde.
So, if you like researching ancient annals,
You'll see even the Romans could not win
Against the Scots, and when the south wind failed
To fend off Rome, and Parthia too fell,
Left just to wither with its fields untilled,
And when the Nile could not bog down Rome's march,
And neither Rhine nor Elbe could chill Rome's heat,
Scotland alone was left, and fought alone,
Defeating Rome. This is the only land
Rome fought with forts instead of mountain ranges,
Fast-flowing rivers, forest borders, deserts.
The Romans needed walls and trenches here.
Though Roman clearances made others exiles
Or slaves, Rome needed northern frontier walls
To keep the Scots' axe-wielding warriors back.
Stopped in its tracks, Rome faltered. Terminus,
The Roman god, marks where Rome turned away
Beside the River Carron, but don't think
Stout hearts used to the warlike work of Mars
Know nothing of the beauties of the arts.
When the barbarians broke the power of Rome
Scotland alone was refuge for the Muses,
Those refugees from wars around the world.
From Scotland Charlemagne brought to the French
Culdees to teach a rising generation
The wisdom of the Classics. Charlemagne
Re-formed the power of Rome as France's power,
Bringing the robe of Romulus to France.
He brokered an alliance with the Scots,
A treaty Mars's sword will never slice,
No rioting or treason will destroy it,
Nor time nor any power known to man
Demolish it. And now that Auld Alliance
Binds closer still and, though you may be proud
Of France's ancient victories against
A world that sought to break the power of France,
Victory came with Scottish soldiers' help.
Whenever Hector's offspring suffered loss
Their Scottish allies shed their own blood too.

Fortunae gens una vices: Francisque minantes
Saepe in se vertit gladios. Scit belliger Anglus,
Scit ferus hoc Batavus, testis Phaethontias unda,
Nec semel infaustis repetita Neapolis armis.
Hanc tibi dat conjux dotem, tot secula fidam
Conjunctamque tuis sociali foedere gentem,
Auspicium felix thalamis concordibus, armis
Indomitos populos per tot discrimina, felix
Auspicium bellis, venturaeque omina palmae.

e
At tu conjugio, Nymphe, dignata superbo,
Te licet et Juno, et bellis metuenda virago,
Et Venus, et Charitum larga indulgentia certet
Muneribus decorare suis, licet ille secundus
Spe votisque hominum Francae moderator habenae
Et solo genitore minor, tibi Regia sceptra
Submittat, blando et dominam te praedicet ore,
Sexum agnosce tamen, dominaeque immunis habenae
Hactenus imperio jam nunc assuesce jugali:
Disce jugum, sed cum dilecto conjuge, ferre:
Disce pati imperium, victrix patiendo futura.
Aspicis Oceanum saxa indignatus ut undis
Verberet, et cautes tumida circumfremat ira:
Rupibus incursat, demoliturque procellis
Fundamenta terens, scopulisque assultat adesis:
Ast ubi se tellus molli substravit arena,
Hospitioque Deum blande invitavit amoeno,
Ipse domat vires, placidusque et se minor ire
In thalamos gaudet non torvo turbidus ore,
Non spumis fremituque minax, sed fronte serena
Littus inoffensum lambit, sensimque relabens

Scotland alone shared always with the French
Fortune's misfortunes, and, as is well known,
It bore the brunt of anger meant for France.
Aggressive England, fierce Batavia
Both know that truth, as do the much invaded
Tough Neapolitans into whose river
Mythology maintains great Phaeton plunged.
Your wife brings you the dowry of a nation
Faithful to France for many centuries,
Linked to your people in a strong alliance,
A happy augury of happy marriage,
A folk never defeated in a fight,
Always an emblem of the winning side.

e
But you, Nymph, worthy of a splendid marriage,
Though Juno and belligerent Minerva,
Venus and the fair, gift-giving Graces
Make you as beautiful as you could wish,
And though the chosen heir to France's throne,
The next director of French government
And second only to the King of France
Should yield a sceptre to you and declare you
Tenderly his equal, you acknowledge
Your place as woman, and so learn to do
His word, setting your own authority
Aside in marriage, but, placing your husband
In charge, learn still to win out through your love.
Learn from the sea that seethes against the rocks,
Cuffs cliffs with anger, beats on headlands, robs
The world's foundations with non-stop typhoons,
Its wave-power wearing down great granite boulders,
But when the land surrenders to the sea
And calls some deity on to the beach
To play, see how the sea draws back his claws,
Delighted to approach this place of union,
This marriage bed of land and sea, not raging,
Not anxious, not with ripping waves and fury,
But with serenity he laps the shore
And seems to kiss it, small waves slipping back

Arrepit facilis cerni, et, ceu mollia captet
Oscula, ludentes in littore lubricat undas.
Cernis ut infirmis hedera enitatur in altum
Frondibus, et molli serpens in robora flexu
Paullatim insinuet sese, et complexibus haerens
Emicet, et mediis pariter caput inserat astris.
Flectitur obsequio rigor, obsequioque paratur,
Et retinetur amor. Neu te jactura relictae
Sollicitet patriae, desideriumque parentis:
Haec quoque terra tibi patria est, hic stirpe propinqui,
Hic generis pars magna tui, multosque per annos
Fortunatorum series longissima Regum,
Unde genus ducis, rerum moderatur habenas.
Quoquo oculos vertes, quoquo vestigia flectes,
Cognatis pars nulla vacat, locus exhibet omnis
Aut generis socios, aut fastis inclyta gentis
Ostentat monumenta tuae. Jam ut caetera mittam,
Hic te, qui cunctis merito praeponderat unus,
Exspectat longe pulcherrimus Hectoridarum,
Pene tibi stirpis communis origine frater:
Mox etiam fratrem quod vincat amore futurus,
Et matrem, et quicquid consanguinitate verendum
Lex facit, et legum quam jussa valentior ulla,
Naturae arcanos pulsans reverentia sensus.
Hic quoque (ni justis obsistent numina votis,
Falsaque credulitas frustra spem nutrit inanem)
Filius ore patrem referens, et filia matrem
Sanguine communi vinclum communis amoris
Firmabunt, brevibusque amplexi colla lacertis
Discutient blando curarum nubila risu.

f
Hunc vitae mihi fata modum concedite, donec
Juncta Caledoniae tot seclis Gallia genti
Officiis, pactisque, et legum compede, fratrum
Subdita dehinc sceptris animo coalescat: et undis

And forwards in a never-done caress
As water takes possession of the land.
Look at how ivy sends its tender leaves
High, high above, spiralling round, embracing
An oak by slow degrees, although a vine
Hugs just as tight and likewise heads towards heaven.
Rigour is sweetened by obedience
And by obedience love is got and held.
Don't let a sense of exile sadden you.
Weep no tears for your mother left in Scotland.
France is your homeland too, and folk from France
Number among your greatest ancestors
Whose line includes blest kings who guided Gaul.
You can't step out your door here without finding
Places your family loved, and good true friends,
Like you, natives of Scotland. All around
Your eye will light on sights famed among Scots.
And, to conclude, this man who waits for you,
The noblest Dauphin, Francis of Valois,
Is Hector's handsomest descendant. He
Will soon be closer to you than a brother,
Mother, or any of your honoured kin,
And stronger than plain legal obligations
Will be the bonds of love joined in your hearts.
So here in France, if God will grant our prayers,
I hope it is no vain and empty hope
A son will come, as noble as his father,
A daughter, apple of her mother's eye,
Making love stronger between two young parents
So children's mischievous and loving faces
Will keep the clouds of care far, far away.

f
Please let the fates let me live long enough
To see Scotland and France, so long drawn close
Through trust, go on to share one government,
Bonded as brothers; and each race whom earth,

Quos mare, quos vastis coelum spatiisque solumque
Dividit, hos populum concordia nectat in unum,
Aequaeva aeternis coeli concordia flammis.

Ad Mariam Illustrissimam Scotorum Reginam

Nympha, Caledoniae quae nunc feliciter orae
    Missa per innumeros sceptra tueris avos:
Quae sortem antevenis meritis, virtutibus annos,
    Sexum animis, morum nobilitate genus,
Accipe (sed facilis) cultu donata Latino
    Carmina, fatidici nobile regis opus.
Illa quidem, Cirrha procul et Permesside lympha,
    Pene sub arctoi sidere nata poli:
Non tamen ausus eram male natum exponere foetum
    Ne mihi displicerant quae placuere tibi.
Nam quod ab ingenio domini sperare nequibant,
    Debebunt genio forsitan illa tuo.

Sea and sky divide across this planet
Unite as one in one true love of concord
Tuned to the timeless concord of the stars.

To the Noblest Mary, Queen of Scots, with a Book of Psalms

Nymph – Mary – Queen of Scots – your throne is yours
Thanks to a legacy of generations
In your royal line, but you transcend them all,
Soaring beyond place, age, sex, royalty
By merit, character, and strength of mind,
So with good grace accept my Latin Psalms,
Translated from that poet-prophet King.
I made them far from the rich port of Cirrha,
Remote from Muses' famed Permessian waters,
Being born beside Killearn, here in the north,
But did not dare abandon these botched offspring
In case I scorned some psalm that you might love;
For what they may not manage through my making
They may yet owe to your ingenious soul.

Magdalanae Valesiae Reginae Scotorum, XVI Aetatis Anno Exstinctae

Regia eram conjux, et Regia filia, neptis
   Regia, spe et votis Regia mater eram.
Sed ne transgrederer mortalis culmen honoris,
   Invida mors hic me condidit ante diem.

Mutuus Amor

   Armata telis dexteram,
Laevam veneno, saeviat
Mors; cuncta tempus demetat
Falce aut senecta deterat:
   Non mortis hoc propinquitas,
Non temporis longinquitas,
Solvet fides quod nexuit
Intaminata vinculum.
   Mors et senectus obruit
Cum Scipione Laelium,
Canam fidem non obruit,
Non pectorum constantiam.
   Durabit usque posteris
Intaminata saeculis
Sincera quae Britannidas
Nectit fides Heroidas.
   Rerum supremus terminus
Ut astra terris misceat,
Regina Scota diliget
Anglam, Angla Scotam diliget.

Madeleine of Valois, Queen of Scots, Dead at Sixteen

Royal wife, royal daughter, royal granddaughter,
I hoped and prayed to be a royal mother,
But lest I seemed like one of the immortals
Jealous death proved me mortal, all too soon.

The Bond of Love

Steel in her sword hand, poison in her left,
Let death rant on, and old age scythe
All down at harvest. Neither death nor age
Will break this bond fidelity has bound.
Though death and age felled those proverbial friends,
Laelius and Scipio, not death nor age
Conquered the constant loyalty in their hearts.
The heart-bond binding Britain's noblest women
Will live unbroken through the generations,
So, though apocalypse fuse earth with stars,
The Queen of Scots will always love
The English Queen, the English Queen
Will love the Queen of Scots.

D. Gualtero Haddono
Magistro Libellorum Supplicum
Serenissimae Angliae Reginae

Frustra senectam, Haddone, provocas meam
    Laeta ad juventae munia,
Musasque longo desides silentio
    Arenam in antiquam vocas.
Aetas choreis cum vigebat aptior,
    Et lusibus decentior,
Vix me in Britannis montibus natum, et solo
    Inerudito et seculo,
Rarae audiebant, rarae adibant fontium
    Deae sacrorum praesides:
Nunc, cum capillis sparserit canentibus
    Declivis aetas tempora,
Cum pulset annus pene sexagesimus,
    Animique langueat vigor,
Surdus roganti Phoebus aurem denegat,
    Musae vocantem negligunt.
Nec Phyllidis me nunc juvat flavam comam
    Praeferre Bacchi crinibus,
Nec in Neaerae perfidam superbiam
    Saevos Iambos stringere.
Nec si quis olim stimulus ingenio additus
    Animum excitabat languidum.
Sed, missionem cum senecta flagitet
    Justam, valetudo imperet,
Libens quiesco, et acquiesco legibus
    Pejoris aevi aheneis:
Tibique, cui sors liberali dextera
    Opes, honores, otium,
Natura mentem vegeto adhuc in corpore
    Diviniorem indulserit,
Applaudo, solum quod queo, magno gradu
    Parnassi ad alta culmina
Feliciore aetate eunti et alite,
    Et enthea vi pectoris.

To Lord Walter Haddon,
Petition Master of the Most Serene Queen of England

No point, Haddon, calling a man my age
   Back to all the fun of teenage years,
No point regrouping long-disbanded Muses
   Back at the old site of a classic gig.
Even when songs were songs and I was stronger
   And love songs seemed to better suit the time,
The Muses hardly bothered about Britain's
   Rough mountains where, in rough times, I was born.
The sacred guardians of the sacred spring
   Beat no path to my front-door in Killearn.
Now when my combed-back hair is turning silvery
   And I will never be the man I was,
When I am someone well-nigh sixty-something
   And the *sang-froid* of my spirits starts to sag,
Apollo won't reply to my petition,
   The Muses hear my whine and turn their backs.
Now I no longer snare blonde singletons
   Instead of snuggling with a single malt,
Nor dash off sonnets with a poison pen,
   Venomous to sting that flirt Neaera –
No, not even when lust reheats years-old
   Embers of poems, going through the motions ...
But since there's a right way to face retirement
   And not being well enforces that right way,
I just square up to things, I make the best
   Of having reached the squarest time of life.
But, look at you! All I can do is cheer
   At how things have worked out: career, awards,
Time to relax. You've the proverbial
   Gift of the gods: *mens sana in corpore sano*,
As you accelerate right to the top
   Of Mount Parnassus, happy and bighearted.
For if a burned-out brain like mine comes out
   With inconceivable sweetness, then I owe it
To Mary, Queen of Scots, my Muses' sponsor,

Nam si quid olim effoeta mens felicius
    Nunc temere fundat, id Deae,
Cui nostra Musa dedicata est, debeo,
    Non viribus mei ingeni.
Haec est Thalia nostra, nostri pectinis
    Haec est magistra et arbitra,
Quae sola Phoebo digna cantat, et cani
    Est digna Phoebi barbito,
Aut alia, si qua barbito Phoebi parem
    Nostrae Deae aequat barbiton.
Quod si Dearum utrinque mentes copulet
    Amica vis concordiae,
Sermone qui nunc vix pedestri repo humi,
    Plebeia fingens carmina,
Arcana rupis Delphicae silentia,
    Situque longo squalidos
Tripodas movebo, et masculo dicam sono
    Jucunda pacis otia:
Dicam Gravidum vinculis coercitum,
    Legum coactam injuriam
Parere frenis, vim repressam et aurei
    Beata secli commoda.
Et nostra si quid audiendum vox dabit,
    Laudi Dearum serviet,
Virtute quarum pax agros Britanniae,
    Urbes fides, fora aequitas,
Et templa pietas, impiis erroribus
    Procul relegatis, colet.

And not a whit to my imagination.
She is our Thalia, lady and fair judge
   Of all our lyrics and of all my art.
Her songs alone are worthy of Apollo,
   And well worth an Apollo with grey hair;
Then there's one other, surely, sings as well
   As that great lady, equalling Apollo,
The most serene Elizabeth of England,
   Haddon, that Queen whose courtier you are,
And if the friendly face of harmony
   Attunes the thoughts of these two sovereigns,
Then I, whose words have aching, fallen arches
   That hirple through my rough, plebeian songs,
Will sing with such a deep sound that the hush
   Of Delphi shall ring out in time of peace
Lightheartedly – I'll make the cauldron wobble
   And all the dust of ages blow away.
I'll sing of wars not breaking out but bound
   In bonds of peace that leash injustice in
Within the law, paying homage to that law
   And the bright blessings of the Age of Gold.
If my voice heralds anything worth hearing,
   Then it will praise these Queens, these Goddesses,
Through whose power peace falls on the fields of Britain,
   Fills British towns with faith, courts with fair play,
And kirks with godliness, while all ungodly
   Error's deported, swept from Britain's shores.

Rogero Aschamo Anglo

Aschamum exstinctum patriae, Grajaeque Camoenae,
   Et Latiae vera cum pietate dolent.
Principibus vixit carus, jucundus amicis,
   Re modica, in mores dicere fama nequit.

E Graeco Simonidis

De luce cassis cor memoriam non supra
Unum tenebit, si cor habeamus, diem.

Ad Henricum Scotorum Regem

Caltha suos nusquam vultus a sole reflectit,
   Illo oriente patens, illo abeunte latens:
Nos quoque pendemus de te, sol noster, ad omnes
   Expositi rerum te subeunte vices.

For Roger Ascham, Englishman

Latin and Greek as well as English Muses
Mourn Roger Ascham with respectful love.
Staunch friend to royals, royal to his friends;
Fame cannot speak of him without a boast.

From the Greek of Simonides

For just one day, all day, the heart remembers
The dear departed, if the heart is wise.

To Henry Darnley, King of Scots

The marigold nowhere turns from the sun.
Opening at dawn, it closes in the dusk.
We too depend on you, our sun. To all
Your turns of fortune we are left exposed.

In Syllam

Nulla cadaveribus quod crux vacet, aut cruce campus,
    Quod lacera in portis omnibus ora patent:
Quod sonat attrita feralis compede carcer,
    Squalet et humanis ossibus albet ager:
Artibus his Regem dici te, Sylla, severum,
    Et patriae affectas ut videare pater.
Sic mihi se medicus doctum per funera jactet:
    Sic fracto laudes Automedonta jugo:
Navita naufragiis celebretur: perdere cives
    Sit laus egregii saeva per arma ducis.
Perdere non populum generosi est gloria Regis:
    Pro populo Regem est gloria vera mori.

Laurentius Valla

Monstra animi domuere sophi: quae terra vel Orcus
    Protulit, Herculea sunt superata manu.
Portentis Latium sermonem Valla levavit,
    Invicto expugnans pectore barbariem.

Against Sulla

No cross without its crucified, no field
Without its cross. In the country of hacked faces
Jails are loud with noise from chains and shackles,
Ploughed hectares are a killing-field of bones.
Do you want to win the title 'Razor King',
Sulla, with your mad act, so you'll be called
Il Duce, Father of the Land? If so,
Rank doctors by who butchers the most patients,
Give drivers prizes for each fatal crash;
When a ship goes down with all hands, praise its captain;
Promote great generals for burning up
Their fellow citizens in dirty wars.
True leadership's not wasting your own people –
The real king gives his own life for *das Volk*.

Lorenzo Valla, Humanist

Like Hercules, wise men culled the mind's monsters.
They won against the worst of earth and hell:
So Valla fought the barbarous in language
And saved pure Latin, thanks to his pure heart.

from De Sphaera

from LIBER I

Quam variae mundi partes, quo semina rerum
Foedere conveniant discordia, lucis et umbrae
Tempora quis motus regat, aestum frigore mutet,
Obscuret Solis vultum Lunaeque tenebris,
Pandere fert animus. Tu qui fulgentia puro
Lumine templa habitas oculis impervia nostris,
Rerum sancte parens, audacibus annue coeptis:
Dum late in populos ferimus tua facta, polique
Immensum referamus opus: gens nescia veri
Ut residem longaque animum caligine mersum
Attolat coelo, et, flammantia moenia mundi
Dum stupet, et vicibus remeantia tempora certis,
Auctorem agnoscat, tantam qui robore molem
Fulciat, aeternis legum moderetur habenis,
Consilio innumerosque bonus conformet ad usus.

from LIBER V

Macti animi, heroes, seclis melioribus orti,
Qui primi ingenii nixi pernicibus alis,
Perque leves vecti stellas, totque orbibus orbes
Implicitos, magni intrastis penetralia coeli,
Naturae in latebris caussas ratione sagaci
Detexistis, et in caeca caligine mersi
Certa ostendistis terris vestigia veri.
    Non caeca ambitio vobis, non blanda voluptas,
Non vigiles curae, non lucri pallida tabes,

On the Planet

from BOOK I

This poem is to show how different
The universe's parts are, and explain
In a unifying theory its discordant
Primordial elements. I set out here
The movement that controls the day and night,
That makes heat alternate with cold, and darkens
The sun's face and the moon's with moving shadows.
O God, the sacred parent of all being,
You who live in regions bright with light
Where human eyes can't reach, sanction this bold
Project to outline to the planet's peoples
All you have made, and while we try to scan
Your *magnum opus*, bless us, so we humans,
Ignorant of the truth, may raise sky-high
Our plodding, unenlightened intellects,
And, as the human mind's amazed to see
The planet's stellar zones, and how the seasons
Recur in their great predetermined course,
The mind may sense the Author of it all,
Who powers the mass of matter with his strength,
Controls it with his everlasting laws,
And who by his sure plan makes it conform
To an infinity of good designs.

from BOOK V

Master minds, born in a better age,
Spirits whose nimble intellectual wings
First flew you through light stars, then through so many
Circles within circles to go deep
Into the furthest reaches of deep space –
You risked all, but, in doing so, detected
The utmost utmost origins of nature,
Your reason guided you across vast floods
And pointed out the stepping stones of truth
Through pitch-dark mirk. Not blind ambition,
Not sexual love, not worry, sleeplessness,
Nor the drained sickness of the profit motive

Sublimes fregere animos, quin invia rerum
Sensibus humanis mentis penetraret acumen,
Eque Deum arcanis adytis per secula longa
Astrorum erueret cassas interprete leges.
Ergo nec imperium vos formidabile lethi,
Nec quae cuncta domant longis oblivia seclis,
Sub latebrisque suis et caeca nocte coercent;
Sed procul obscuri tenebris ab inertibus Orci
Gloria sublimes illustri in luce reponet,
Praepetibusque vehet per postera secula pennis.

Broke your strong spirit. Quick wit's acumen
Took you instead inside creation's secrets,
To distant wildernesses human sense
Can't reach without the mind, and from the hidden
Sanctuaries of the gods, year after year
You first teased out the laws that rule the stars.
So you will not be cowed by Lethe's empire
Nor by oblivion which locks up aeons
In the eternal blackout of blind night;
But, far from Orcus' empty dark, bright glory
Will sheath you in pure light, carried away
On wings of mounting speed towards times to come.

Ioannis Calvini Epicedium

Si quis erit nullos superesse a funere manes
Qui putet, aut si forte putet, sic vivit ut Orcum
Speret et aeternas Stygio sub gurgite poenas,
Is merito sua fata fleat, sua funera ploret
Vivus, et ad caros luctum transmittat amicos.
At nos, invitis quamquam sis raptus amicis
Ante diem, magnis quamvis inviderit ausis
Mors, te flere nefas, Calvine, et funera vanae
Ludibrio pompae et miseris onerare querelis.
Liber enim curis, terrenae et pondere molis,
Astra tenes, propiusque Deo, quem mente colebas,
Nunc frueris, puroque vides in lumine purum
Lumen, et infusi satiatus numinis haustum
Exigis aeternam sine sollicitudine vitam;
Quam neque deiciunt luctus nec tollit inani
Ebria laetitia spes exanimantve timores,
Quaeque animo offundit morbi contagia corpus.
Hanc ego, quae curis te lux exemit acerbis,
Natalem iure appellem, qua raptus in astra
In patriam remeas, et post fastidia duri
Exilii, mortis iam mens secura secundae,
Fortunae imperio maior, primordia longae
Ingreditur vitae. Nam ceu per corporis artus
Cum subiit animus, pigrae vegetatque movetque
Molis onus, funditque agilem per membra vigorem;
Cum fugit, exanimum iacet immotumque cadaver,
Nec quicquam est luteae nisi putris fabrica massae:
Sic animi Deus est animus, quo si caret, atris
Obruitur tenebris, specieque illusus inani
Fallaces rectique bonique amplectitur umbras.
Ast ubi divini concepit numinis haustum,
Diffugiunt tenebrae simulacraque vana facessunt,
Nudaque se veri facies in luce videndam

Elegy for John Calvin

If anyone dreams death is just the end,
Or thinks souls live, but lets his life invite
Hell's unremitting Stygian punishments,
Then he's quite right, at the mere thought of dying,
To howl in middle-age, and clutch his friends;
But, though you have been snatched away too soon
From your own folk, kidnapped by jealous death
Who envied your astonishing career,
Calvin, it would just mock you to drown out
Your funeral with stagey wails and cries.
For you have jettisoned the weight and care
Of life on earth. Your home is in the stars.
In heaven you see up close the selfsame God
You saw here with your inner eye, pure light
Housed in pure light. So now, your great thirst slaked
With drinking deep drafts of the Holy Spirit,
You relish perfect everlasting life,
Neither cast down by grief, nor in high hope
Of vain, deceptive joy, and not laid low
By scares and the infection of disease
With which the body clouds the human spirit.
I know I'm right to call yon day a birthday
When you left pain, hauled off into the stars,
Where, home again, after your trials of exile,
Secure from any further fear of death,
Beyond the power of fortune, you turned over
A new, long life. In the same way as when
A soul starts coursing through a body's limbs,
Quickening their vegetative weight,
Letting new life kick in; and just as when
A soul leaves a cadaver lying like clay,
And there is nothing left but one dead lump –
So God is the soul's soul, and without God
Come only blackouts, empty simulacra,
Untrue illusions of the good and true.
But when the soul communes with God's own soul
Darkness dissolves, mere simulacra vanish,
The naked face of truth glows in the light

Exhibet aeterna, quam nullo vespere claudit
Saepta caput furvis nox importuna tenebris.
Hunc ergo in portum caelo plaudente receptus
Tu licet in placida tranquillus pace quiescas,
Non tamen omnino potuit mors invida totum
Tollere Calvinum terris: aeterna manebunt
Ingenii monumenta tui, et livoris iniqui
Languida paullatim cum flamma resederit, omnes,
Religio qua pura nitet, se fundet in oras
Fama tui. Ut nuper falso te nomine Clemens,
Te Pauli duo, flagitiis et fraude gemelli,
Te Iuli timuit rabies, te nobilis una
Fraterna impietate Pius: sic nominis umbram
Ingeniique tui effigiem post fata timebit
Vana superstitio; quique olim in sede Quirini
Triste furens flammaque minax ferroque tyrannus
Transtulit inferni cuncta in se munia regni,
Imperio Pluto, foedis Harpyia rapinis,
Eumenis igne, Charon naulo, triplicique corona
Cerberus, immissi stupefactus lumine veri,
Terrificoque tuae deiectus fulmine linguae,
Transferet infernas in se post funera poenas:
Inter aquas sitiens, referens revolubile saxum,
Vulturibus iecur exesus, cava dolia lymphis
Frustra implens, Ixioneum distentus in orbem.

Of an unending day which no bleak night
Cloaked in long gloaming shadows can put out.
So, though great cheering crowds across the heavens
Welcomed you into port where you may rest
In peace and calm, envious death could not
Wipe every trace of Calvin from the earth.
The monuments of your ingenious spirit
Will last forever. When, little by little,
Meanminded flames of jealousy die back,
Your reputation will reach every shore
Where true religion shines. As, recently,
No-clemency Clement, that dire pair of Pauls
(The Devil's Duo), crazy Julius, Pius
Notorious for his impiety –
As they all feared you, so, after your death,
The image of your genius and your name
Will haunt and terrify all superstitious
Airheads. Every pope who used to rant
And rave on Romulus's Roman throne,
Each fancy Führer with his fire and sword
Who made himself a minister of Hell,
A power-mad Pluto, a heart-crushing Harpy,
A martyr-burning Fury, a ferryman
Flogging indulgences, a Cerberus
In triple papal crown, will now be blasted
By the terrifying thunder of your teaching,
And, immolated in the light of truth,
Call down on his dying self the fires of Hell:
He'll thirst and thirst with cool drinks all around him,
He'll roll and roll the Sisyphean rock,
He'll have his liver ripped apart by vultures,
He'll go mad trying to fill a sieve with water,
Be racked, full-length, on Ixion's burning wheel.

Ad Theodorum Bezam

Praesul optime, sacra Christiana
Qui caste colis et facis, canisque,
Ad te carmina mitto, nec Latino
Nec Grajo sale tincta, sed Britannis
Nata in montibus horrida sub Arcto,
Nec coelo neque seculo erudito.
Quae si judicio tuo probentur,
Ut classis modo in ultimae referri
Possint centurias, nihil timebo
Censuram invidiae, nihil morabor
Senatus critici severitatem,
Nihil grammaticas tribus: mihi unus
Beza est curia, censor et Quirites.

To Theodore Beza

Swiss friend, Calvin's successor, playwright, poet,
True Christian in your worship, life, and art,
Here are my poems, hardly at all steeped
In Greek or Latin *nous*, but British-made
On cold bens under dim, crude British stars.
Still, if you think maybe because you like them
They'll stand examination by professors,
I'll risk green-eyed reviews and not put off
My Judgement Day of grammar and lit crit.
For me, though, just one special readership
Matters on earth, and, Beza, you are it.

Hymnus Matutinus ad Christum

Proles parentis optimi,
Et par parenti maximo,
De luce vera vera lux,
Verusque de Deo Deus:

En nox recessit, jam nitet
Aurora luce praevia,
Coelum solumque purpurans,
Et clausa tenebris detegens.

Sed fuscat ignorantiae
Caligo nostra pectora,
Et nubilis erroribus
Mens pene cedit obruta.

Exsurge sol purissime,
Diemque da mundo suum:
Nostramque noctem illuminans
Erroris umbram discute.

Dissolve frigus horridum;
Arvumque nostri pectoris,
Calore lampadis tuae,
Humore purga noxio.

Ut irrigetur coelitus
Roris beati nectare,
Et centuplo cum foenore
Coeleste semen proferat.

Morning Hymn to Christ

Undisputed Son of God,
Peer of your peerless Parent's might,
Heavenly Father's only Son,
True light begotten of true light!

Instead of darkness now here comes
Daybreak ushering in day
To let the great rays of the sun
Blaze on what darkness held at bay.

Still, though, the haar of ignorance
Casts a shadow on the brain
And under its misleading fog
The urge to give in grows again.

So, rise, you purest sun of all
And give this world your light of day,
Shining across our human night
And chasing error on its way.

Rid us of the freezing cold
And give our souls soul-food to eat
So all that's poisoning our minds
Gets burned away by your lamp's heat.

May the brain be nourished now
By the blessed heavens' dew
Until the rich mind's heavenly crops
Are reaped a hundredfold for you.

In Iulium II Pontificem

Genua cui patrem, genitricem Graecia, partum
   Pontus et unda dedit, num bonus esse potes?
Fallaces Ligures, et mendax Graecia, ponto
   Nulla fides. In te singula solus habes.

In Eandem Romam

Non ego Romulea miror quod pastor in urbe
   Sceptra gerat, pastor conditor urbis erat.
Cumque Lupae gentis nutritus lacte sit auctor,
   Non ego Romulea miror in urbe Lupos.
Illa meum superat tantum admiratio captum,
   Quomodo securum servet ovile Lupus.

Ite, Missa Est

Ire licet: missa hinc quo debuit ire remissa est.
   Nempe ad Tartareum trans Phlegetonta Patrem.

Oan Paip J 2

Daddy a Genoan, Mammy a Greek,
Yer a fushionless son o the sea.
Tallies, Greeks, an the Med are full o lyin cheek.
You, pal, are full o aa three.

The Pope of Rome Again

No surprise a shepherd bears the sceptre
In Romulus's city. After all,
A shepherd founded it. And as that founder
Sooked milk from a wolf's teat, so, no surprise,
Rome's full of wolves. What really gets me, though,
Is how a wolf can find work as a shepherd.

Go, Mass is Over

Time to go: time for the Mass to go
Over the Firth of Flame to the Pope of Hell.

Imago ad Peregre Venientes Religionis Ergo

Fare age qui terras lustras vagus hospes et undas,
    Quid petis hinc? Longae quae tibi caussa viae?
Non Deus hic quisquam, nec imagine numen in ista est,
    Nos lapis et tantum putria ligna sumus:
Vermibus esca, cibus tineis, domus hospita blattis,
    Opprobrium coeli, ludibriumque soli.
Non capiunt humiles numen coeleste penates,
    Structa nec humana saxea tecta manu;
Quem mare, quem tellus, quem non capit igneus aether,
    Clauditur in nullo spiritus ille loco.
Ut Christum invenias, animi secreta revolve,
    Aut lege fatidici quae cecinere patres:
Aut quae dives habet passim circumspice mundus,
    Haec vera est aedes, hoc penetrale Dei.
At quisquis picto gaudet dare basia trunco,
    Crassaque pulvereo lingere saxa croco,
Dignus morte perit, qui mortua vivus adorat,
    Et vitae in fragili spem sibi ponit humo.
Si te picta juvant, cariem ne perline trunci,
    Sed vera mentem simplicitate tuam,
Hac ratione domi poteris reperire, quod omnes
    Erro vagus terras sic peragrando fugis.

The Image to the Pilgrims

Pilgrim, whose home's so long been homelessness,
Trekker across far lands and passenger
Ferried across the waves, what are you after?
There's no God here, nothing but rotting wood,
Worm-food, moth-food, a creepy-crawly bughouse
Scorned by the sky, made fun of by the sun.
No tabernacle human hands have raised
Or graven image holds the soul of God.
God's soul that soars above earth, sea, and sky
Is not pinned down in one specific place.
If you seek Christ, find him in your own mind's
Remotest glens or the prophetic fathers'
God-given words, or let your eyes locate
Plenitude within the whole wide world.
This is the true kirk, God's own tabernacle,
But folk who slobber kisses on mere daubed
Tree trunks, or lick dust-coated yellow rocks,
Die as they ought who act as if base matter
Mattered more than being alive. What's painted
May please the eye, but give up daubing tree trunks.
Instead, do something simply for the soul's sake,
Then what you search for, tramping round the world,
You may find when you look in your own home.

ARTHUR JOHNSTON

from Musarum Elogia

URANIA

Astra vides istic, Phoebeis aemula flammis,
    Nata Lycaonii pene sub igne poli.
Ante tegebantur: nebulas nunc Scotus et umbras
    Discutit, et donat perpete luce frui.
Quantus hic est, ipsis lucem qui fenerat astris?
    Hunc socium certe Phoebus honoris habet.

EUTERPE

Hic Scoti congesta manu Fergusia cernis
    Sidera, quae tenebris mersa fuere prius.
Tota micat stellis pars caeli dextra, sub illa
    Sideribus pariter Scotia tota nitet.
Sidera sideribus confer: non omnibus illa,
    Astra Caledoniae gentis ubique micant.

CALLIOPE

Vatibus Arctoae gentis Tarvatius heros
    Et lucem et vitam, quam meruere, dedit.
Hos simul ostendit mundo, disparuit ingens
    Turba Poetarum, visa nitere prius.
Quam meruit laudem? Quae vitam mille Poetis
    Attulit, haec eadem dextera mille necat.

THALIA

Vidimus ambrosio saturatos nectare flores
    Itala quos, et quos Celtica fudit humus.
Cernimus hic quos terra tulit vicinae Bootae,
    Terra pruinosa sub cane tecta nive.
Est fecunda quidem tellus, quae protulit illos,
    Qui tulit hos Scotis, est mage cultus ager.

Four Muses' Sentences

for Sir John Scot of Scotstarvit,
Judge, and Sponsor of the Anthology of Scottish Latin Poets

URANIA

See these dead brilliant Apollonian stars
Lighting the north, these stars were clouded over
By fog-bound blackout, non-stop polar drizzle,
Till you came, firing up your blaze of glory,
Phoebus's right-hand man, lender of light,
Scots star of Apollo, Scotstarvit.

EUTERPE

Here in your book are the bright sparks of Scotland,
Ancestral fireflies long pronounced extinct.
Constellated up there flash by flash,
A country-wide *aurora borealis*
Flames our broad mearns, but these, your gathered stars,
Shine on all lands their stellar poems' light.

CALLIOPE

Light and new life are tough Scotstarvit's gift
To torchlit poets of a northern land
Who now burn bright, but when their light flares out,
Others, once seen as clear, will be eclipsed.
This same right hand rekindling these dead poets
Throttles as many who had hoped to live.

THALIA

After the nectar-splattered, orchidaceous
French and Italian stuff, pick out here now
Under the dogstar's numbing, grouse-white snow
Arcturan flowers. The Continent
Outburgeons us, but thin-soiled offshore Scotland
Gets for its flowers a bonus of hard graft.

Edinburgum

Comminus ut spectet superos caeloque fruatur,
    Montis in acclivi surgit Edina iugo.
Ancillatricem Cererem Nymphasque ministras,
    Et vectigalem despicit inde Thetin.
Hic ubi nascentis se pandunt lumina Phoebi,
    Sede sub Arturi regia tecta vides,
Solis ad occasum surgens, arx imminet urbi:
    Haec habet Arctoi tela tremenda Iovis.
Adspicis in medio templum, decus urbis et orbis,
    Hac pietas stabilem fixit in aede larem.
Cuncta nitent intus; regalis more coronae
    Plexilis aurato marmore lucet apex.
Virginis Astraeae domus est contermina templo,
    Digna Polycleti Praxitelisque manu.
Tecta colunt cives solis heroibus apta,
    Nullius illa minas, nullius arma timent.
Albula Romuleam, Venetam mare territat urbem,
    Quas regit, undarum ridet Edina minas.
Crede mihi, nusquam vel sceptris aptior urbs est,
    Vel rerum domina dignior urbe locus.

Edinburgh

So she can see directly into heaven
Edinburgh rises on her rock
Whose view commands the rich kingdom of Ceres,
Her train of nymphs, the tributary sea.
East, in the sunshine of the young Apollo,
A palace glints just below Arthur's Seat;
Where the sun sets the castle rules the city
Armed with the northern thunderbolts of Jove.
From the town's heart the high kirk beams its message
Urbi et orbe, fixed in its true faith;
Spectacular inside, St Giles's spire
Is crowned with a corona of carved stone.
Well worth Praxiteles or Polycletus,
The law courts of Astraea stand next door.
The people live in fine homes fit for heroes.
They fear no threat. No force of arms unnerves them.
The Tiber frightens Rome, the sea scares Venice,
But Edinburgh smiles at all such fuss.
Believe me, nowhere more deserves a sceptre,
No town on earth's more suited to command.

Glasgua

Glasgua, tu socias inter caput exseris urbes,
    Et te nil ingens pulchrius orbis habet.
Sole sub occiduo Zephyri te temperat aura,
    Frigora nec brumae, nec Canis ora times.
Glotta latus cingens electro purior omni est,
    Hic regis imperio lintea mille tuo.
Pons iugat adversas operoso marmore ripas,
    Et tibi securum per vada praebet iter.
Aemula Phaeacum tua sunt pomaria silvis,
    Ruraque Paestanis sunt tibi plena rosis.
Farra Ceres, armenta Pales, Thetis agmina gentis
    Squamigerae, nemorum dat tibi Diva feras.
Tecta nitent, ipsas et tangunt vertice nubes;
    Quo commendentur, plus tamen intus habent.
Templa domos superant, radiant haec marmore puro,
    Marmoris et pretium nobile vincit opus.
Non procul hinc Themidis se tollunt atria, patres
    Hic ubi purpureos dicere iura vides.
In medio residens sua pandit limina Phoebus,
    Hic cum Permesso Pegasis unda fluit.
Civibus ingentes animos Deus armiger, artes
    Nata Iovis, stabiles Iuno ministrat opes.
Moenia Dardanidum posuit Grynaeus Apollo,
    Et Deus aequoreis qui dominatur aquis.
Glasgua, te fausto struxerunt sidere Divi,
    Quot mare, quot tellus, quotquot et aether habet.

Glasgow

Head held high among sister cities,
Glasgow, you are a star.
Gulf Stream winds defrost you. No fear, though,
Of your being frazzled to a crisp at high noon.
The Clyde sweeps through, detoxed like amber,
A thousand ships flying your flag.
Ashlar bridges you, bank to wet bank,
Granting all comers safe passage.
Round about, orchards and roses
Up the Clyde Valley, a Paestum of the distant west,
Woodnymphs each lithe as a salmon.
Town centre tenements' flashbulb brilliance
Hides wall-to-wall Style; sheer marble
Churches to die for. Down the road
Rat-a-tat patter stuns the Sheriff Court.
Bang in the middle, your University
Sings hymns to Phoebus Apollo.
You make the gods grin, my favourite Glasgow.
Sea, earth and air have ganged up to make you shine.

Sterlinum

Sterlino quis digna canat? Cunabula Reges
    Hic sua securis imposuere iugis.
Aura salutifera est, facit hoc vicinia coeli,
    Nec datur a saevo tutior hoste locus.
Adspicis hic geminis structas in rupibus arces,
    Tectaque Tarpeii turribus aequa Iovis.
Fortha triumphales hic, dum fugit, excipit arcus,
    Cogitur et curvo subdere colla iugo.
Haud aliter Phrygiis ludit Maeander in oris,
    Saepe fluit trepidans, saepe recursat aqua.
Orbe perrerrato levis huc vestigia flectens
    Advena miratur ruris et urbis opes.
Admiranda quidem sunt haec, et carmine digna,
    Plus tamen hic virtus Martia laudis habet.
Non semel Ausonios Sterlinum reppulit enses,
    Limes et Imperii, quem bibit amnis, erat.

Stirling

Who can do Stirling justice? Cradle of kings
Who set their castle strong on its high ridge,
Its fresh air keeps that great outpost of heaven
Secure there, safe from enemy attack.
Towering on its matched rocks, its own towers match
The towers of Jove by Rome's Tarpeian Rock.
Nobly the River Forth lets itself flow
Underneath two fine triumphal arches.
Hesitantly, often turning back,
Winding like Phrygia's River Maeander,
It moves with a light touch, and takes its time.
The town and country smile, gifted with riches,
But Stirling's fame in war is even more
Worth epic celebration. More than once
This place repelled the spears of Rome, its river
Commanded Rome's imperial eagle, *Stop!*

Andreapolis

Urbs sacra, nuper eras toti venerabilis orbi,
　Nec fuit in toto sanctior orbe locus.
Iuppiter erubuit tua cernens templa, sacello
　Et de Tarpeio multa querela fuit.
Haec quoque contemplans Ephesinae conditor aedis,
　Ipse suum merito risit et odit opus.
Vestibus aequabant templorum marmora mystae,
　Cunctaque divini plena nitoris erant.
Ordinis hic sacri princeps, spectabilis auro,
　Iura dabat patribus Scotia quotquot habet.
Priscus honor periit; traxerunt templa ruinam,
　Nec superest mystis qui fuit ante nitor:
Sacra tamen Musis urbs es, Phoebique ministris,
　Nec maior meritis est honor ille tuis.
Lumine te blando, Musas quae diligit, Eos
　Adspicit, et roseis molliter afflat equis.
Mane novo iuxta Musarum murmurat aedes
　Rauca Thetis, somnos et iubet esse breves.
Proximus est campus, studiis hic fessa iuventus
　Se recreat, vires sumit et inde novas.
Phocis amor Phoebi fuit olim, Palladis Acte:
　In te iam stabilem fixit uterque larem.

St Andrews

Sacred St Andrews, the whole wide world
Saw you as the burgh of God.
Jove, eyeing your great Cathedral,
Blushed for his own wee Tarpeian kirk.
The architect of the Ephesian temple,
Seeing yours, felt like a fake.
Culdee priests in holy cassocks
Gazed through your East Neuk of light.
St Andrews' Archbishop, clad in gold,
Bellowed at Scotland's Parliament.
Now that's gone, walls ankle-high,
Priestly *fiat lux* tarnished.
Still you pull poets, though. You wow
Lecturers and lab technicians.
Aurora of the peep o' day in Fife
Frisks ashore with salt-reddened fingers,
Herring-sparkle of dawn.
Thetis coughs through 10 a.m. haar,
Waking hirpling, hungover students
Who sober up with golf clubs.
Phocis was Phoebus's long-time lover,
Attica of Pallas. In St Andrews
Each dances. Forever. Now.

Taodunum

Urbs vetus, undosi cui parent ostia Tai,
    Et male Cimbrorum quod tegit ossa, solum,
Genua te spectans sua ridet marmora, moles
    Pyramidum flocci barbara Memphis habet.
Ipsa suas merito contemnunt Gargara messes,
    Quasque regit, damnat terra Liburna rates,
Et Venetum populi de paupertate queruntur,
    Nec Cnidus aequoreos iactat, ut ante, greges.
Si conferre lubet, pubes Spartana iuventae,
    Consulibus cedit Roma togata tuis.
Qui mendicatum Tai de gurgite nomen
    Dat tibi, credatur mentis et artis inops.
Structa Deum manibus cum possis iure videri,
    Iure Dei-donum te tua terra vocat.

Dundee

Veteran admiral of the windy Tay,
Commanding a great Firth whose shores stretch out
To where invading Vikings left their bones,
The marble palaces of Genoa,
The pyramids of Memphis, count for nothing
Compared to you. You trump all Gargara
For sheer abundance, and for seamanship
Out-sail Liburnia, Cnidus, even Venice.
Your boys are braver than the lads of Sparta.
Your councillors out-argue even Rome's.
Only the ignorant pretend your name
Derives prosaically from Dun Tay;
Your true root's far more nimbly classical:
Dundee, Dei Donum, God's Gift.

Mons Rosarum

Nobilis urbs rosei iam gaudet nomine montis,
    Quae prius a caelo dicta Celurca fuit.
Proximus huic mons est, quem praeterlabitur amnis;
    Ambrosias populo praebet uterque dapes.
Mons lectas pecudes, salmones sufficit unda,
    Lautius et si quid stagna Neronis habent.
Quae recreent oculos, incingunt lilia ripas,
    Ipsaque puniceis sunt iuga picta rosis.
Ad latus eoum se vectigale profundum
    Explicat, et velis mille teguntur aquae.
Propter aquas populo praebet spectacula campus,
    Flumine quem Boreas hinc lavat, inde Notus.
Hic iuvenum pars flectit equos, pars utitur arcu,
    Pars rotat Herculea grandia saxa manu.
Sunt quos lucta iuvat, pars gaudet ludere disco,
    Vel volucres curvo pellere fuste pilas.
Urbs celebris, te si spectet, Capitolia Romae
    Iuppiter, Idalium deseret alma Venus.

Montrose

Previously celestial Celurca,
This noble town is now called *Monte Rosa*.
A river inundates its sheltering hillside,
River and hillside keep its folk well-fed.
Pedigree cattle roam the hill, and salmon
Make the river rich as Nero's ponds.
A sight for sore eyes, lilies light the banks,
While the surrounding slopes glow with red roses.
Eastwards, the North Sea pays Montrose its tribute,
Dancing with innumerable sails.
Bathed by both the South Esk and the North,
Yon public park, The Links, is a broad meadow
Where the town's youngsters come to race their horses,
Or practise archery, or putt the shot
With arms like Hercules's. Some play quoits,
Wrestle, or hit a small ball with hooked clubs.
Venus would come here from her home on Ida.
If Jupiter could see Montrose from Rome's
Capitol, he'd emigrate here too.

Brechinum

Fertile Brechinum geminos interiacet amnes,
  Hic Boream spectat, respicit ille Notum.
Rupibus inclusae sternuntur pontibus undae,
  Sunt quoque securis flumina plena vadis.
Hanc simul Arctoi decorat victoria regis,
  Perfida cum socii terga dedere duces.
Praesulis hic sancti domus est, et pyramis aedi
  Proxima, Phidiacae forsitan artis opus.
Si molem spectes, nihil est exilius illa,
  Ipsa tamen caeli culmina tangit apex.
Est structura teres, nec raro lumina fallit,
  Eminus hanc spectans esse putabis acum.
Daedala compages et ventos ridet et imbres,
  Nec metuit magni tela trisulca Iovis.
Si fabricam conferre lubet, Brechinia turris
  Pyramidas superat, Nile superbe, tuas.

Brechin

Fertile Brechin lies between two rivers,
One the South, the other the North Esk.
Multiple bridges span these rivers' waters,
And many fords let people safely cross.
A northern lord fought here and won, when allies
Took to their heels. A bishop's holy kirk
Stands right beside a tapering round tower
Phidias might have shaped with his own hand.
Though tourists see that campanile as slender,
It soars sky-high. From miles away it shines
Bright as a needle. Yet for centuries
It's laughed off wind, downpours, and lightning strikes.
Should anyone set up a competition,
Brechin would beat the Pyramids of Nile.

De Aberdonia Urbe

Cum populo quisquis Romanam suspicis urbem,
    Et mundi dominam deliciasque vocas;
Confer Aberdoniam, Thetis hanc servilibus undis
    Alluit, urbs famulo nec procul illa mari est.
Utraque fulta iugis subiectos despicit amnes;
    Utraque fulminea spirat ab arce minas.
Illa suos Fabios, invictaque fulmina belli
    Scipiadas iactat, Caesareamque domum.
Mennesios urbs haec proceres, gentemque Culenam,
    Et Collissonios, Lausoniosque patres.
Urbe Quirinali minor est urbs Grampica, cives
    Sunt tamen hic animis ingeniisque pares.

On the City of Aberdeen

If you think Rome's the world's clear Number One,
Consider Aberdeen. That city too
Is bathed by Thetis's obedient waves
In much the way that Rome's sea washes Rome.
Both towns grandly survey their subject rivers,
Both fulminate and girn in their Town Halls.
As Rome reels off its roll of undefeated
Proud Fabii and Scipios and Caesars,
So Aberdeen recalls with pride her Menzieses,
Her Cullens and her Collisons and Lawsons.
Romulus's city may be bigger
Than the *urbs Grampica*, but Aberdeen
Has citizens whose hearts are big as Rome's.

Elginum

Laudibus Elgini cedunt Peneia Tempe,
   Et Baiae veteres, Hesperidumque nemus.
Hinc maris, inde vides praedivitis aequora campi,
   Frugibus haec populum, piscibus illa beant.
Huc sua Phaeaces miserunt poma, Damasci
   Pruna nec hic desunt, vel Cerasuntis opes.
Attica mellifici liquistis tecta volucres,
   Et iuvat hic pressis cogere mella favis.
Aemulus argento fecundos Loxa per agros
   Errat et obliquis in mare serpit aquis.
Arcibus Heroum nitidis urbs cingitur, intus
   Phoebeii radiant nobilumque lares.
Omnia delectant, veteris sed rudera templi
   Dum spectas, lacrimis, Scotia, tinge genas.

Elgin

Praised beyond Baiae, Tempe, or the grove
Of the Hesperides, the town of Elgin
Enjoys the endless largesse of the sea
Eastwards, and rich, broad farmlands to the west.
Here the Phaeacians sent their native apples.
Damascus sent her ripest damson plums,
And Ceralus the Black Sea's very best.
From Attica a colony of bees
Flew here. Its honeycombs are heathered nectar.
The Lossie winds like silver through lush fields,
Gently meandering to the North Sea.
Nobles have built grand, Apollonian mansions
Inside the town, and all round it's surrounded
By shining castles of heroic chiefs.
Everything's beautiful, except one building:
Elgin cathedral with its ancient glory
Ruined. Scotland, look at that, and weep.

from Nobiles Scoti *and from* Episcopi Scoti

MARRIUS

Inter Areskinus proceres nitet, aurea flammas
   Inter ut aethereas Luna micare solet.

LOVETIUS

Natus hyperboreos inter Fraserius heros,
   E spinis docuit surgere posse rosam.

CARNEGIUS

Nec numero clauduntur opes, nec limite rura
   Carnegi, servat mens tamen alta modum.

ABREDONENSIS

Enthea Forbesio mens est, vox consona menti,
   Vita comes vocis: quod iubet, ipse facit.

GALLOVIDIENSIS

Lammius astrorum spoliatus lumine, lucem
   Qua se, quaque Deum conspicit, intus habet.

LISMORENSIS

Quot pater Amphion, et quot Rhodopeius Orpheus,
   Mellifluo Bodius tot trahit ore feras.

Scots Lords, Scots Bishops

ERSKINE OF MAR

As the moon like mica shines among the stars
So Erskine shines among the other Lords.

LOVAT

A Fraser from the hyperborean north
Has shown that out of thorns can spring a rose.

CARNEGIE

Carnegie's wealth and lands cannot be counted,
Yet his pure mind maintains the middle way.

FORBES OF ABERDEEN

Forbes' mind is a true gift of God. His voice
Matches his mind. Each thing he says, he does.

LAMB OF GALLOWAY

Lamb, who can no longer see the stars,
Sees God in his own soul through inner light.

BOYD OF LISMORE

Boyd's sweet voice calls as many feral creatures
As Amphion or Rhodopian Orpheus.

De Anatomica Sectione, a Iulio Casserio Placentino Patavii Exhibita

Felices animae, quarum, plaudente theatro,
    Secta Placentinus corpora monstrat eques.
Vestra ille aeternum victuris nomina chartis
    Inseret, et laudes orbis uterque leget.
Mortalis sin vita placet, descendite caelo,
    Corpora restituent quae secuere manus.

De Reginae Choreis

Nuper erat Boreae constrictum frigore caelum,
    Flumina vincta gelu, rura sepulta nive.
Aethera nunc Zephyris mulcentur, puppibus unda
    Sternitur, et laeto gramine vernat humus.
Ipsa tuis, Princeps, applaudunt astra choreis,
    Et reliquus tecum gaudia mundus agit.

On an Anatomical Dissection Exhibited at Padua by Julius Casserius of Placentia

Happy souls whose bodies are cut up
In public here by Julius of Placentia,
The theatre's audience gives you a cheer.
Your names, cadavers, will be written down
And last forever, so both hemispheres
Will read your praises listed in old scrolls.
Still, if you'd rather live, pop back from heaven,
Consult this surgeon, and you'll find yourselves
Set right by these same hands that cut you up.

On the Queen's Dances

Last month the sky was locked up in hard frost.
Ice chained the burns. The farms were deep in snow.
But now the air is full of benign breezes,
The sea is calm for ships, earth bright with green.
It is the stars, Princess, praising your dances,
The world's on holiday, to dance with you.

De Comite Hollandio

Adspice quam studiis vitam traducat ineptis
   Aulicus, accipitres hic alit, ille canes,
Una saginat equos, gaudet pars una choreis,
   Iste genas fuco purpurat, ille mero.
Hunc pugil, hunc meretrix emungit et histrio nummis,
   Sunt quibus et pernox alea vastat opes.
Altius assurgit generosi sanguinis heres,
   Richaeus, Clariae captus amore lyrae.
Quas colit, auratis Musas hic protegit alis,
   Gaudet et Aonio dicere iura choro.
Hunc dictatorem sequitur Parnassia pubes,
   Fertque suo supplex debita tura duci.
Reddite Pierides Flaccum, revocate Maronem,
   Iam Maecenatem terra Britanna tulit.

On the Earl of Holland

Consider all the daft ways courtiers
Find to pass the time: one pampers horses,
Rears hawks, or hounds, or falls in love with dance.
One gets red-cheeked with rouge and one with wine.
One's been completely fleeced by some tough boxer,
Or by an actor, or a shrewd wee whore.
But Baron Rich, heir of a generous race,
A true highflier, loves Apollo's lyre.
He guards the Muses with his gilded wings
And loves to ask for the Aonian choir.
The young Parnassians fete him as their Prince,
Offer him incense, down on bended knees.
Muses, please bring back Horace, bring back Virgil,
Now we've a real Maecenas in our midst.

Insignia Equestria Divi Georgii

Quisquis Hyperborei spectas insignia Regis,
    Sub Iove nil illo grandius esse puta.
Quis neget hunc Martis furias contemnere, cuius
    Pectus eques ferro protegit, igne draco?
Quis neget huic servire Deos, cui crura Cupido
    Ornavit spoliis exuviisque Deae?
Terrarum imperio quis dignum nesciat illum,
    Quem scapula caeli sidera ferre vides?

De Columbario Eudoxi Praesulis

Quas aluit templo turris vicina, columbae
    Praesulis antiquos deseruere lares.
Non strigis has solitis exegit pupula nidis,
    Nec mustelarum perniciosa cohors;
Nec pelagi murmur, nec tintinnabula templi
    Proxima, nec strepitus praetereuntis aquae;
Nec circumvolitans magni Iovis armiger ales
    Linquere Chaonias tecta coegit aves;
Rostra nec accipitris metuerunt: sola volucres
    Cypridis austeri praesulis ora timent.

Insignia of the Knights of Saint George

Whoever sees the northern king's insignia
Thinks there is nothing grander in this world.
An English knight who wears St George's breastplate
Is strong inside its steel, and kept secure
By dragon's fire so that he can spit upon
The rage of Mars. Everyone knows the gods
Are good to any true Knight of St George.
That knight holds tokens given him by Cupid:
Knight of the Garter is his other name.
None can deny he's fit to rule the planet
Who wears the stars of heaven sewn on his scarf.

Bishop Eudoxus' Doocot*

Fessed-up in yon tower by the high kirk
The Bishop's cushie-doos hae fleed awa.
Whit flegged thaim wisnae howlets, wisnae vile
Paircels o whittricks, wisnae bullerin seas,
Wisnae yon kirk's bells *tintinnabula*,
Nor the hush or whush o wattir rinnin by.
Nae aigle o Jove nor onie gled wis dreed.
The puir wee burdies o the goaddess Venus
Wer aa afeard o yon dour Bishop's snoot.

---

* Doocot – *dovecot*; fessed-up – *reared*; cushie-doos – *doves*; flegged – *frightened*; howlets – *owls*; paircels – *gangs*; whittricks – *weasels*; bullerin – *roaring*; neist – *next*; hush/whush – *rushing sound*; aigle – *eagle*; gled – *hawk*; dreed – *feared*; snoot – *face*.

De Balagaunio Eiusdem Equo

Tempora si numeres, senio Balagaunius omnes,
 Pascua qui tondent Scotica, vincit equos.
Hunc ego crediderim Mario vel consule natum,
 Pergama vel Graio cum periere dolo.
Pes piger est illi, macies in corpore toto,
 Et solitos duro respuit ore lupos.
Hunc tamen ut scandit Gordonus, fulminis ignes
 Cogit et alipedes antevolare Notos.
In sene Ionstono Musas cum suscitet Heros,
 Quid mirum est vetulis si dominetur equis?

Ad Illustrem Comitem Gordonium, Marchionis Huntlaei Filium, Natu Maximum

Dum proprius Nemetum premeret Gordonius urbem,
 Glande sibi figi sensit ab arce femur.
Dum Nymphae thalamos idem sibi destinat Heros,
 Pectus Acidaliae cuspide figit Amor.
Urbe triumphata rediit, nisi sidera fallunt,
 Porriget et victas Nympha petita manus.

Balagaunius

Count up the years: that Balagaunius
Must surely be the oldest horse in Scotland.
I just about believe he was a foal
Either in Marius's consulship
Or when the Wooden Horse went into Troy.
Arthritic now, he stands thin as a rake.
His stubborn jaws reject the jagged bit.
But when the Earl of Gordon mounts him, *he*
Makes him course faster than a lightning strike
Or some wing-footed zephyr of the south.
When the heroic Earl of Gordon wakes
The muse of praise in ageing Arthur Johnston,
Small wonder that the selfsame Earl of Gordon
Shows an old warhorse how he's still in charge.

To the Illustrious Earl Gordon, Eldest Son of the Marquis of Huntly

At the grim siege of Speyer a musket ball
Fired from the citadel pierced Gordon's thigh
When he pressed on too hard, and that same hero,
Pursuing hard his lovely bride-to-be,
Found his heart pierced by Venus's sharp arrow;
But just as he returned victorious
From Speyer, so too, unless the stars deceive,
The girl he seeks will let his hands win out.

De Eiusdem Lapsu ex Equo

Laedere Gordonum lapsu qui nequiter audes,
    Quid tibi non optem, saeve caballe, mali?
Exue cum freno phaleras et ephippia, tergum
    Nemo paret strigili comere, nemo iubam.
Indue clitellas posthac et iunctus asello
    Verte molam, plaustrum vel trahe, more bovis.
Non potes armenti generosi pullus haberi,
    Bellua, tardigradi gloria prima gregis.
Non iuga te Scythiae, non te tulit Africa tellus,
    Nec quae nobilibus claruit, Astur, equis.
Ditis equi, Nycteus, Aethon, Orphnaeus, Alastor,
    Ad vada Tartarei te genuere lacus.
Pegasus excusso domino conscendit Olympum,
    Ad stabulum Stygii te decet ire Iovis.

On the Fall of the Earl Gordon from his Horse

Wild horse whose bucking threw the young Earl Gordon,
There is no punishment you don't deserve.
Off with your saddle, bridle, all your trappings:
Let no comb comb your straggly mane or back.
From now on you'll wear panniers, and snort,
Paired with a donkey, pulling round some mill,
Or haul a cart as if you were an ox.
You can't be treated like some thoroughbred,
Brute beast, prime duffer of the also-rans.
No Scythian or pure Moroccan stallion
Sired you. You're no top-notch Asturian steed.
Your stablemates are stalled in deepest Dis –
Nycteus, Aethon, Orphnaeus, Alastor –
For Tartarus is where you were a foal.
Pegasus climbed to heaven, minus his master,
But you should gallop back right down to hell.

De Gulielmo Gordonio Rothimaeo, et Georgio Gordonio Caesis

Gordonii cecidere duo discordibus armis,
　Ambo senes, iuvenum ductor uterque fuit.
Miscuit hos primos Mavors, mors abstulit unos,
　Evasit comitum, sorte favente, cohors.
Fortunam ex sociis, ex his audacter in hostem
　Ducere, constanter disce, iuventa, mori.

On William Gordon of Rothiemay and George Gordon, Killed in Action

In the discord of the fight
Two Gordons died.
Each in old age
Captained brave youths.
Mars caught them first;
Death carries each
Away alone.
Their lucky troops
Escaped this time.
Learn those troops' luck,
And from the Gordons
How to attack
Courageously,
And, young men, learn
With total dedication
How to die.

De Iohanne Gordonio, Vicecomite de Melgein, et Iohanne Gordonio de Rothimay in Arce Frendriaca Combustis

Vos supremi ignes, extremaque lumina mundi,
Insomnesque faces, et ponto nescia mergi
Sidera, mutatae monumenta perennia formae,
Magna minorque ferae, custosque Erymanthidos Ursae,
Quique Lycaonias circum Draco pervigil Arctos
Adspicis, Herculeis olim confixe sagittis,
Astraque vos praeter si quae Fergusia tellus
Cernit in occiduis semper vigilantia flammis,
Edite, nam testes vos, et nox conscia facti
Exstitit, Arctoi nuper sub cardine caeli;
Gordoniae quis, vasta movens incendia, gentis
Torruit heroas, feta truculentior ursa,
Impastoque lupo, nec tigride mitior, icta
Dum furit, aut rapta dum saevit prole leaena?
Vidimus et diris opprobria barbara flammis
Addita. Mausoli poterant qui busta mereri,
Pyramidas vel Memphi tuas, vel Porsena si quid
Altius erexit, postquam deferbuit ignis,
Vilibus illati stabulis iacuere iugales
Inter equos, putri stipula foenoque sepulti.
Nec mora, tosta focis et adhuc fumantia mensas
Corpora texerunt, imae spectacula plebi.
Hic proceres cum plebe iacent, discrimine nullo.
Effigies his nulla viri est, sua brachia nulli,
Nil humeros supra, nil est sub pube relictum:
Cuique suus tantum superest sine nomine truncus.
O caelum, O Superi! Post haec quis regis equile
Threicii, dirasque feri Busiridis aras,
Aut Laestrygonias epulas, aut foeda Thyestae

The Atrocity at Frendrocht

where John Gordon, Viscount of Melgum (Lord Aboyne) and John Gordon of Rothiemay were burned in the Tower of Frendraught on the night of 8 October 1630

High fires of the night sky, remotest lights
That never sleep and cannot quench yourselves,
Memorials of metamorphoses,
Greater and lesser Bear, bright, mile-high dragon
Pierced by the arrow-tips of Hercules
Vigilantly hunting for Callisto,
And stars, if you are visible from Scotland,
Staring forever on the western fires –
Identify, since you were witnesses
Last night beneath the pivot of the sky,
That murdering fire-raiser who immolated
Clan Gordon's heroes; signal who hit harder
Than pregnant bear or hungry wolf, no gentler
Than a gashed, lashing lioness or tigress
Maddened at the seizure of her cubs.
We've seen the mutilation that was part
Of the attack, so those who should have had
A Mausoleum or a pyramid
Like that at Memphis, or the tomb set up
By Porsena, lie strewn around instead
After the blaze, among dead plough-horses
Felled in their stables' dirt, buried beneath
Hay bales and rotting stubble. Right away
Corpses like blackened meat lay smouldering
Spread out on planks for everyone to gawp at,
Masters and servants all reduced to one.
   The bodies look inhuman. Armless. Faceless.
Nothing below the crotch. Only the torso
Of each is left. No more. None has a name.
I swear by heaven's breadth and by the gods,
No one who's seen this will be shocked again
By the shit and meat of the Augean stables,
Busiris's wild altars, or those cannibals
The Laestrygonians; not by Thyestes
Devouring all his children, nor that meal

Prandia, quaeque Iovi fertur struxisse Lycaon,
Aut tua crudelis miretur fercula Progne?
Innocuos iuvenes, patriis in finibus, inter
Mille clientelas, et avito sanguine iunctos
Hospitii dominos, omnis damnique dolique
Securos, somnoque graves, et noctis opacae
Vallatos tenebris, animatis sulphure flammis
Vidimus exstinctos, et tracta cadavera foedis
Indignisque modis, postquam sunt ultima passi.
Tristis, et infelix, et semper inhospita turris
Momento succensa brevi, simul ima supremis
Miscuit, et tumulos thalamis, et funera somno,
Et famulis dominos, quorum confusa iacebant
Obruta ruderibus cinis, ossa, cadavera: namque
Corporis unius, memini, pars ossa fuerunt,
Pars cinis immundus, tostum pars igne cadaver.
Quam sors dura fuit! Vivos dum pascitur ignis,
Nemo manu, prece nemo iuvat, nec abire parantes
Quisquam animas pius ore legit, vocesve supremas
Aure bibit, dextra vel lumina condit amica.
Nemo sacra cineres turbatos excipit urna.
Nemo parentales lacrimas insontibus umbris,
Aut trucibus dat tura rogis, aut serta sepulcris.
Illustres iuvenes, procerum genus alter, avito
Alter Hyperboreos attingens sanguine reges,
Sic pereunt, stratique iacent florentibus annis.
Ah prius hoc procerum par inclarescere mundo
Debuerat, patriamque novis implere tropaeis,
Seu domito, quem tota hominum gens odit, Ibero,
Sive triumphatis aquilis Rhenoque bicorni,
Gordoniae quem gentis honos, Huntleius heres,
Imperio nunc Celta tuo, circumsonat armis
Undique Grampiacis, et sanguine miscet herili.
Debuerat fratri comitem se iungere frater,

Some say Lycaon fed to Jupiter,
Nor, Procne, by how you served up your own son.
Now we have seen right here at Frendrocht Tower
How harmless young men lying down among
Their clansfolk, sleeping in ancestral Forgue
Surrounded by their local childhood friends
Who gave and shared true hospitality,
Tired out, not bothered about death or plots,
Underneath the blackness of the night
Were soon asphyxiated by the smoke
From thick, sulphurous flames, those harmless boys
Tortured, and then their corpses dragged and dumped.
   That inhospitable, bleak, lowering tower
Was burned down in an instant, its top storey
Collapsing inwards, crashing to the ground,
Fusing the wedding chamber with the grave,
Death with sound sleep, masters with servants, ashes
Of human beings with smashed bones and rubble.
The body parts were indistinguishable
From one another and from ash. When fire
Feeds on live flesh there is no hope, no prayer,
No parting kiss, no overheard last word.
No friendly fingers lightly closed their eyelids.
No one should die like that: no relatives
To take away the loved one in an urn,
No friends to stand by weeping for their souls,
Or offer incense as the pyre flares up,
Or lay a wreath. There aren't even graves.
   Two well-known lads, both from good families,
One a descendant of the Northern kings,
Died in this way, so sickeningly young.
They should have won another kind of fame,
Filling their native land with great, fresh trophies,
Fighting as soldiers to beat back yon Spaniards
The whole world hates, or scoring victories
Against the eagles and the twin-horned Rhine –
That's where the Celtic glory of Clan Gordon
And the name Huntly radiate with power,
The arms of Grampian all around, at one
With officers' blood. Each boy should have joined up,

Cognatusque latus cognati cingere, pugnas
Inter et arma ducum, maioraque fulmina belli.
Sed decus hoc nostris invidit Tartarus oris,
Tartarea vel gente satus; nam criminis huius
Horruit aspectu tellus, et pontus, et aether.
Aemula maiorum soboles, quae nescia vinci,
Nescia terreri frameas spernebat et enses,
Fraude perit tectisque dolis, nec cernitur hostis.
O saeclum, O mores! Fuit olim gloria gentis
Grampigenae nescire dolos, sed viribus uti,
Et conferre manus, campisque patentibus armis
Cernere fulmineis, et sternere comminus hostem.
Sic domiti Pictique truces, Cimbrique feroces,
Sic Tibris et dominae repressa potentia Romae est,
Nec secus armorum princeps et gloria Vallas,
Quique Caledonias rexit feliciter oras
Brussius, Hayorum comitatus principe, vastos
De sibi vicina pepererunt gente triumphos.
Heu, nunc orba viris, et plusquam degener aetas,
Rem gerit insidiis, Martis pro cuspide sica est,
Toxica pro telis, et clandestinus ubique
Pro iaculis, Bellona, tuis, heu, spargitur ignis;
Auctorem nec scire datur; secretior ille est,
Quam pelagi fontes aut incunabula Nili.
   Sacra cohors, cui iura Themis legesque supremas
Credidit, et scelerum comites Rhamnusia poenas;
Ardua si iuvenum virtus, et sanguis in uno
Regius, orborum vel praematura parentum
Canities, viduusque torus miserabilis Hayae,
Si iuris, si gentis honos, vel gloria saecli,
Te movet, irato pietas vel debita caelo,
Da trucis artificem sceleris. Quod poscimus aequum est.
Iudicis officium est causas aperire latentes,

Brothers in arms, kin next to kin, away
Soldiering across the battlefields of Europe,
Daring every thunderbolt Jove throws;
But Tartarus, or one of that dour Ilk,
Begrudged our shores such glory, and so earth,
Sea, and sky now shudder at this crime.
Each boy, an equal of his ancestors,
Unbeatable, bravehearted, making light
Of swords and claymores, meets his death in this
Atrocity, this cowardly attack.
    O saecula! O mores! It was once
The glory of the Grampian race to know
No guile, to use sheer strength, to enter in
To combat out on open fields, to fight
With force of arms, and close in for the kill.
That's how the Picts were conquered, and the Cimbri,
And how even the Roman Tiber's power
Was turned aside. Centuries later, Wallace
And Robert Bruce's prosperous command
Kept Scotland strong – thanks to the family
Of Hay threats close to home were beaten off.
But this is now no age for manliness.
Ours is a time past decadence, a sly
Era when the sword's swapped for the dirk,
Arrows for poison, and across the land
Where once Bellona's javelins were hurled,
Terrorists strike instead. Nobody knows
Who to arrest. The culprit's more elusive
Than where the sea starts or the Nile begins.
    You great courts of our nation, to whom Thetis
Consigned the rule of law, and Nemesis
The rightful penalties to punish crime,
If these two butchered boys were nobly brave,
If one came of royal blood, or if the shocked,
White faces of his parents and the widowed
Lady Hay can move you; if there's still
Respect for law or clan or glory here
Or duty owed now to the outraged heavens,
Show us who did this. What we ask is right.
It is the duty of the judge to probe

Qua licet, et scelerum primos exquirere fontes,
Et modo blanditiis, duris modo vocibus uti,
Omnia tentando, lex quae permittit et aequus
Iuppiter: exigui levis est iactura laboris.
Omnibus excussis vi, iudex, scire quod optas,
Extorquere potes; praesto est qui vellicet artus
Simius, et stridens non uno culeus angue.
Est tibi traiectis armata ciconia nervis,
Est rota, sunt fustes, et iniquo pondere torquens
Ancora cervices, et quae premat ocrea suras.
Utque, quod admisit, dirum scelus expiet, ultor
Nunc sceleris, famulos praebebit Mulciber ignes.
Scotigenae ne gentis honos, sanctique Senatus
Gloria foedetur, poenis ultricibus insta:
Ure, seca, nulloque virum discrimine saevi,
Dum tormenta tibi, superest dum Scotica cervix.

For hidden truth wherever possible,
And to investigate the origins
Of crime with subtle questions and with harsh
Interrogations using all the force
Of justice Jupiter allows. Proceed.
No effort's wasted. Through investigation,
Using coercion, judge, you can extract
The information: you have implements
To tear limbs, you have drugs, and snakes in sacks.
You can make use of implements of torture,
The wheel, the clubs, the ankle-crushing 'boot'.
Eager to condemn what he permitted,
Vulcan has allowed you now to use
His red-hot branding iron on suspects' flesh.
Don't let the honour of the Scottish people,
The glory of its parliament, be tarnished.
Find who did this. Burn. Cut. Spare no one
You can torture, while there still remains
A single Scottish throat left to be slit.

from Ad Robertum Baronium

Adspice, Gadiacis quod misi tristis ab undis,
    Baroni, plenum rusticitatis opus.
Urbe procul, parvus, nec sat fecundus agellus
    Est mihi, saxosis asper ubique iugis.
Hic ego, qui Musis olim Phoeboque litavi,
    Devotus Cereri praedia bobus aro.
Curvus humum spectans, interdum pone iuvencos
    Sector, et impresso vomere findo solum.
Interdum stimulo, nec raro vocibus, utor,
    Et stupidum numeros discere cogo pecus.
Nunc subigo rastris, nunc terram crate fatigo,
    Horrida nunc duro tesqua bidente domo.
Hic manus exossat lapidosa novalia, lymphis
    Hic rigat inductis, hic scrobe siccat humum.
Saepe flagellatae lassant mihi brachia fruges,
    Ambo fatigantur saepe ligone pedes.
Ipse lutum nudus furca versare tricorni
    Cogor, et immundo spargere rura fimo.
Vere novo videas mandantem semina sulcis:
    Arva sub Arcturi sidere falce meto.
Pars messis torrenda focis, fragendaque saxo est,
    Pars mihi flumineis mersa domatur aquis.
Aestibus in mediis, hiemis memor, ignibus apta
    Pabula suffossa quaerere cogor humo.
Viscera dum rimor terrae, prope conspicor umbras,
    Ignotum nec me Manibus esse reor.
Ingeminant curae, ceu tempestate coorta,
    Cum prior urgetur fluctibus unda novis.
Vix intempesta clauduntur lumina nocte,
    Excitor, ut cecinit nuncia lucis avis.

To Robert Baron

Dear Doctor Baron, Aberdeen,
Read this, my mudstained, gloomy work
Sent from a burn that feeds the Don.
Out on my croft, far out of town,
Among rough, stony, worn-out fields,
Ex-poet and ex-learned man,
I plough my furrow with dour beasts.
Bent double, eyes glued to the clods,
I trek behind my oxen's lines,
Goading them on or chanting verse,
Teaching the ox boustrophedon.

Sometimes I hoe and hoe the marl,
Sometimes I harrow it to death,
Or jab it. With my writing hand
I haul the stones from new-ploughed fields
Then, maybe, irrigate the land,
Or drain it with a shallow pit.
Both arms ache with threshing crops,
Both feet are just about done in.
Stripped off, I fork muck with a graip,
Then spread dung on the heavy soil.
Arcturus winks. I scythe my crops.

Some of the harvest's scorched, ground down,
Some of it's in the Gadie Burn.
Through the hot summer I prepare
For snow, cutting and banking peat.
Excavating the earth's bowels
I just about see spooks and think
The dead peer back. What makes it worse,
As when a storm first hits and then
Wave after wave pounds in, my head's
Just touched the pillow in pitch dark
When I'm awoken by the lark.

Pellibus hirsutis humeros involvo pedesque:
　Rapa famem pellit, fluminis unda sitim.
Mille modis pereo; nil infelicius, uno
　Me miserabilius nil gravis Orcus habet.
Me mea nunc genitrix, et quae dedit ubera nutrix,
　Horreret: vultu terreor ipse meo.
Non ego sum, quod eram: foedantur pulvere cani,
　Ora situ turpi, crura pedesque luto.
Obstipum caput est, et adunco suetus aratro
　Semper humi figo lumina, more bovis.

My overalls are shaggy pelts.
Breakfast's a turnip once again,
The Gadie Burn to wash it down.
I'm dying in a thousand ways –
The Underworld might cheer me up –
So lonely, scared the mirror shows
Not who I was. Teeth like a dog's,
Hair dandruff-white, boils on my lips,
I take my stand knee-deep in shite,
Bowed-down, too harnessed to the plough,
Downcast, the beast I have become.

In Obitum M. Davidis Balantini de Kinnochar, Ecclesiastae

Falce Balantinus fatali concidit, aevi
   Sex properans rapidis claudere lustra rotis.
Vera simul periit pietas et quidquid honesti,
   Quidquid et ingenuae mentis in orbe fuit.
Fugerunt Charites, fugerunt Palladis artes,
   Cultus et eloquii cum gravitate nitor.
Liquit opes aliis: virtutes ille paternas,
   Quas coluit, secum vectus in astra tulit.
In quoscunque lubet posthac, Mors improba, saevi,
   Sive paras homines figere, sive Deos.
Utere fatali nullo discrimine ferro,
   Et quate funereas tristis ubique faces.
Delicias hominum rapuisti, pessima rerum:
   Ulterius feritas tendere nulla potest.

On the Death of the Reverend David Ballantyne of Kilconquhar

Death's scythe has cut down David Ballantyne
Before time raced him to the age of thirty.
True piety died with him, and all honour,
All innocence remaining in this world.
Gone are the Graces, the Palladian arts,
The cultured gravitas of eloquence.
He willed his goods to others, but those good
Paternal qualities he cherished most
Have vanished with him to beyond the stars.
Sadistic Death, whether you mean to kill
Humans or gods, kill on and show no mercy.
Cut down any or all, and hurl around
Funeral torches grimly everywhere.
Death, lowest of the low, has culled our finest.
No further cruelty could outdo this.

Ad Iamisonum Pictorem, de Anna Cambella, Heroina

Illustres, ars quotquot habet tua, prome colores,
    Pingere Cambellam si, Iamisone, paras.
Frons ebori, pectusque nivi, sint colla ligustris
    Aemula, Paestanis tinge labella rosis.
Ille genis color eniteat, quo mixta corallis
    Marmora, vel quali candida poma rubent.
Caesaries auro rutilet: debetur ocellis,
    Qualis inest gemmis sideribusque, nitor.
Forma supercilii sit, qualem Cypridis arcus,
    Vel Triviae, leviter cum sinuatur, habet.
Sed pictor suspende manum; subtilius omni
    Stamine, quod tentas hic simulare, vides.
Cedit Apollineo vulsus de vertice crinis,
    Cedit Apellea linea ducta manu.
Pinge supercilium sine fastu, pinge pudicos
    Huic oculos, totam da sine labe Deam.
Ut careat naevo, formae nil deme vel adde,
    Fac similem tantum, qua potes arte, sui.

To Jamesone the Artist,
About the Splendid Lady Anne Campbell

Your palette needs as many glowing colours
As you can muster now, George Jamesone,
If you would paint the lovely Lady Campbell.
Ivory brow and breasts of snow, a neck
Like privet flowers, her lips miniature roses
From Paestum, and the colour in her cheeks
Is coral mixed with marble, or the glow
Of ripest apples; eyes sheer gems or stars.
Her eyebrow the eyebrow of Aphrodite
Or of Diana – bow-like, nimbly curved.
But stop there, painter. There's something much subtler
Than you could ever see or copy here.
The god Apollo highlighted her hair.
Apelles sculpted each expressive hand.
Put no pride in her eyebrow. When you paint her,
Paint modest eyes, flawless and goddess-like.
For if you aim to make a perfect picture,
You only have to paint her as she is.

Tumulus Nobilissimae Heroinae, Annae Cambellae, Marchionissae de Huntley

Erige Cambellae tumulum de marmore puro,
    Hic ubi Lichtoni Praesulis ora vides.
Incumbat Phrygiis moles operosa columnis,
    Et Mausolei nubila tangat apex.
In medio sculpenda Dea est, quae crinibus aurum,
    Sidera luminibus, pectore vincat ebur.
Coniugis Huntlaei iuxta caeletur imago,
    Martia fulminei quae gerat ora ducis.
Candida nobilibus varientur marmora gemmis,
    Et spoliis Rubri Sidoniique maris.
Congere sapphiros, adamantas, iaspides, ignes
    Et quos chrysolithus, quosque pyropus, habet.
Nec nitor argenti desit, nec divitis auri,
    Quod legit in patriis gens Peruana iugis.
Ars pretium superans formet sine labe toreuma,
    Phidiaca dignum Praxitelisque manu.
Optima quae rerum fuit, et pulcherrima, tali
    Promeruit tumulo vel meliore tegi.

The Tomb of the Noblest Heroine Anne Campbell, Marchioness of Huntly

Build for Anne Campbell a pure marble tomb
In Bishop Lichton's aisle, St Machar's Kirk.
Let the sophisticated structure stand
On Phrygian columns, and her mausoleum's
Apex graze the clouds that pass above.
A goddess must be sculpted in the centre,
Her hair outshining gold, her eyes the stars,
Breasts ivory white. And let her husband,
Huntly, have his image carved close by,
So she can see her brave lord's martial face.
Variegate the veins of the pale marble
With noble gems, trophies from the Red Sea
And from the Sea of Sidon. Then heap up
Diamonds, jaspers, fiery chrysolites
Or bright pyropuses. Omit no gleam
Of silver or rich gold that the hill people
Gather on their far Peruvian bens.
Let art add its invaluable value
To a faultless masterpiece that could have come
From the hand of Phidias or Praxiteles.
Anne, paragon of all worth and all beauty,
Deserves a shrine like this, or better still.

In Obitum Gulielmi Forbesii Cragivarrii

Nobilis hic tumulum Forbesi conspicis; audi
   Qui fuerint mores, ingeniumque viri.
Quod labor est aliis, vitae dum carperet auras,
   Divitias illi quaerere ludus erat.
Cumque iuberetur terris excedere, ridens,
   'Terra vale, caelo nunc potiemur,' ait.
Quas possedit opes et terrae iugera, nemo
   Miretur; dominum plus fuit esse sui.

Obituary for William Forbes of Craigievar

You see the tomb here of a noble Forbes.
Hear how he lived, and what his thoughts were like:
Throughout his life he did not play the game
That others played, for money and career.
When the time came for him to die, he said,
Smiling, 'Fareweel, earth. Aa that is my ain's
Hauden* in heivin noo.' Do not admire
His wealth or his estates, for he well knew
To be the lord of his own self was finer
Even than being the Laird of Craigievar.

* Hauden – *held.*

In Obitum Iohannae Ionstonae

IONSTONUS
Ionstonae thalamo tumulum, taedisque maritis
    Funereas iunxit mors properata faces.
Virgo fuit, cum coepit hiems, cum constitit, uxor,
    Mox gelidus, bruma deficiente, cinis.
Est rota Fortunae volucris, fugitiva voluptas,
    Spes hominum semper lubrica, vita brevis.

WEDDERBURNUS
Ionstono carmen dedit immortale Thalia,
    Quis morti hic facibus funereisque locus?

IONSTONUS
Quod spondes, optare queat, sperare Camena
    Nostra nequit, gelidi sidere tacta poli.

WEDDERBURNUS
An Buchananeae capiunt te oblivia Musae?
    Sidere an hanc nescis incaluisse tuo?

IONSTONUS
Mille tulit, fateor, sub iniquo sidere cygnos,
    Unum Phoenicem Scotica terra dedit.

WEDDERBURNUS
At simul in cinerem Phoenix consederit unus,
    Si qua fides, alium suscitat inde cinis.

IONSTONUS
Tantae molis opus non uno absolvitur aevo:
    Hanc reparant volucrem non nisi saecla decem.

WEDDERBURNUS
Iam vates obiit. Mundo post funera Phoenix
    Redditur, et sobolem dat rogus ipse novam.

On the Death of Joanna Johnston

JOHNSTON

The honeymoon is suddenly a funeral.
The marriage torch turns to a torch of death,
Your death, Joanna Johnston. In your life
You were a young girl at the start of winter,
A wife in winter's depths, and at its end
Ashes. The wheel of Fortune can't be trusted.
Pleasures just as much as human hopes
Remain uncertain. Always. Life is short.

WEDDERBURN

Thalia makes Arthur Johnston's song immortal,
So why this need for funerals and death?

JOHNSTON

Though my Muse hopes her song will never die,
She feels the chill of a cold northern star.

WEDDERBURN

Have you forgotten George Buchanan's Muse
Which shone beneath the same sky as your star?

JOHNSTON

Scotland's harsh star has lit a thousand swans,
But she has given the world one Phoenix only.

WEDDERBURN

But when one Phoenix settles in its ashes,
A second Phoenix rises from that pyre.

JOHNSTON

Such a great process needs more than one era:
A thousand years pass till that Phoenix comes.

WEDDERBURN

Buchanan's dead now. From his funeral pyre
A new Phoenix is born, to match the old.

IONSTONUS

Dispensat summam Lachesis mortalibus horam:
   Credere fas non est, numina posse mori.

WEDDERBURNUS

Si, Ionstone, tibi est Buchananus numen, ab Arcto
   Scotia, te nato, numina plura dedit.

IONSTONUS

Desine, vel patriae, mi Wedderburne, sodalis
   Vel tibi praestrinxit lumina dulcis amor.

JOHNSTON

Only Lachesis sets men's hour of death.
No one should think, though, a great soul can die.

WEDDERBURN

Johnston, if George Buchanan is to you
A great soul, in you Scotland has another.

JOHNSTON

Enough. Some kinsman, ally, or some lover
Has blurred your vision, Wedderburn, my friend.

De Horto Suo

Aemula Phaeacum silvis, pomaria nobis
　In medio surgunt ambitiosa foro.
Hic tristis dum saevit hiems, quae Punica tellus,
　Quaeque ferax mittit Media, poma lego.
Nil opus hic rastris durisve ligonibus, hortus
　Hic domino nullo poma labore parit.
Aureus est hortus nobis, hunc protulit aetas
　Aurea, qua fructus sponte ferebat humus.
Hunc tibi vel ferro vel stercore nata dederunt
　Saecula, quem ferro stercoribusque colis.

De Gulielmo Drummondo

Quaesivit Latio Buchananus carmine laudem,
　Et patrios dura respuit aure modos.
Cum posset Latiis Buchananum vincere Musis
　Drummundus, patrio maluit ore loqui.
Maior uter? Primas huic defert Scotia, vates
　Vix inter Latios ille secundus erat.

My Book Garden

Rivalling the gardens of Alicinous,
My branching fruit trees spread for all to see.
Even in the very depths of winter
I harvest Punic fruits and Persian citrons.
No need for rakes or hoes. My garden grows
Apples for its owner without work.
An eighteen-carat golden garden, given
By a golden age when, once, the soil itself
Spontaneously blossomed. But your garden,
Mechanically tilled, dug with manure,
Comes only from an age of iron and dung.

On William Drummond

George Buchanan sought to rival Virgil.
His perfect ear spurned verse in his own speech.
Drummond, who might have equalled him in Latin,
Used a native language when he wrote.
Who wins? Scotland ranks Drummond first in English,
And holds Buchanan second, after Virgil,
Among all poets in the Latin tongue.

Saltatrix

Adspice, quo tegimur, caelum, quae fata ministrant
    Omnibus: astrorum mente revolve choros.
Nunc properant, nunc lenta meant, nunc stare putantur
    Sidera, retrorsum nunc trepidare vides.
Dissiliunt, coeunt, sidunt, tolluntur in altum,
    Scilicet aethereae pectine mota lyrae.
Hic iuvenum specta choreas, et sidera gyros
    Hic docuisse suos, vel didicisse, putes.

De Hylo Concionatore

Qui dormire paras, nocturna silentia noli
    Quaerere, nec strepitum praetereuntis aquae;
Nec volucrum, nec quos edit lyra tinnula cantus,
    Quaeque soporiferum grana papaver habet;
Nec molli te crede toro, nec membra fatiga,
    Nec dape, nec sumpto lumina conde mero:
Ut sopor obrepat non expugnabilis, audi,
    Dum coram populo rhetoricatur, Hylum.

The Dancing Art

Look up and see the sky that covers us
And allocates a destiny to each.
Catch with your inner eye the choirs of stars.
One moment they speed on, the next go slowly,
Or seem to hover, even judder backwards,
Split up, join together, rise and fall
As if they followed a celestial music.
See these choirs here, these youths, and think the stars
Have learned from them, or taught them all they know.

On the Popular Haranguer 'Hylus' Wood

If you want a really good, sound sleep
Don't choose either the silence of the night
Or the soothing sound of gently flowing water
Or birdsong or the sweet lilt of the lyre
Or granulated-poppy sleeping pills.
No need to go to bed or do exhausting
Workouts or eat and sleep until you drop.
If you want guaranteed, uninterrupted,
Comatose sleep, you only have to listen
To the Public Lectures of a man called Wood.

Inneruria

Urbs dilecta mihi, te mollibus alluit undis,
    Urius, antiquum nomen et inde trahis.
Te quoque Dona rigat cristallo purior, illum
    Mox Gariochaeis Urius auget aquis.
Cur tua Mygdoniis non surgunt tecta columnis,
    Nec radiat titulis Pyramis ulla tuis?
Cur humiles sorbis cinguntur vilibus aedes,
    Sacra quibus potius debita laurus erat?
Ante triumphatus te iuxta Brussius hostem
    Trivit, et ex illo victor ubique fuit.
Nec procul hinc populos Steuarti dextra rebelles
    Fregit et Harlaeam sanguine mersit humum.
Te iactare mihi fas est: quae divite gleba
    Te beat, est cunis proxima terra meis.
Te prope vitales puer hausi luminis auras,
    Te prope, iam canis obsitus, opto mori.

Inverurie

The town I love! Bathed by the gentle Urie
From whose soft waves you take your ancient name.
Crystal-clear, the stately River Don
Flows through, swelled by the Garioch and Urie.
Where are the pyramids of Inverurie?
Why no acropolis to sing your fame?
Here, where there should be laurels, rowans grow.
Nearby, defeated Bruce won his first battle
And, after that, won battles everywhere.
Not far from here too Stewart's strong right arm
Smashed rebel clans on Harlaw's bloodstained clay.
My destiny's to be proud of this place
Where I was born, out on a fertile farm.
Back where I first drew breath, out in the fields
I sink into a dream. This is my choice:
To see Inverurie and die.

De Loco Suo Natali

Aemula Thessalicis en hic Ionstonia Tempe,
   Hospes, hyperboreo fusa sub axe vides.
Mille per ambages nitidis argenteus undis
   Hic trepidat laetos Urius inter agros.
Explicat hic seras ingens Bennachius umbras,
   Nox ubi libratur lance diesque pari.
Gemmifer est amnis, radiat mons ipse lapillis,
   Queis nihil Eous purius orbis habet.
Hic pandit Natura sinum, nativaque surgens
   Purpura felicem sub pede ditat humum.
Aera per liquidum volucres, in flumine pisces,
   Adspicis in pratis luxuriare pecus.
Hic seges est, hic poma rubent, onerantur aristis
   Arva, suas aegre sustinet arbor opes.
Propter aquas arx est, ipsi contermina caelo,
   Auctoris menti non tamen aequa sui.
Imperat haec arvis et vectigalibus undis,
   Et famula stadiis distat ab urbe tribus.
Haec mihi terra parens: gens has Ionstonia lymphas,
   Arvaque per centum missa tuetur avos.
Clara Maroneis evasit Mantua cunis,
   Me mea natalis nobilitabit humus.

Birthplace

Here, neck and neck with the Vale of Tempe,
Stretches the Howe of the Johnstons.
Underneath Aberdeenshire sky
The sparkling, silvery Urie Burn
Slaloms over well-fed farms.
Bennachie's sgurr untousles a last quiff of cloud;
Night and day hang in the balance.
The Don hides garnets. The high glens, too,
Dazzle with gemstones, bright as India's best.
Nature reclines *au naturel*
On a surging bed of heather. Swallows
Loop in tangy air. Salmon
Flicker. Strong-bodied cattle
Chew the cud in the pastures.
Here, where northern apples redden,
Cornfields bend under golden grain,
Largesse lets orchards sag.
I sprang from this, these rivers, fields
Over a hundred generations
Always the Howe of the Johnstons.
Virgil made his birthplace famous;
Mine will be the making of my poems.

Index of Poem Titles

George Buchanan

A Commendation of the *Commentarius* of Diogio de Teive to King João III of Portugal 13
Ad Eandem [Leonoram] 20
Ad Eundem Invictissimum Regem De Hoc Commentario Georgius Buchananus 12
Ad Henricum Scotorum Regem 62
Ad Mariam Illustrissimam Scotorum Reginam 54
Ad Peiridem Lenam 18
Ad Rectorem Scholae Conimbricae Mursam, etc. 8
Ad Theodorum Bezam 74
Adventus in Galliam 30
Against Sulla 65
Against Zoilus 17
Andreae Goveano 6

Beleago 9
Brasilia 16
Brazil 17

Can Damage Your Health 35
Coming to France 31

D. Gualtero Haddono Magistro Libellorum Supplicum Serenissimae Angliae Reginae 58
De Equo Elogium 32
De Sphaera (extract) 66
De Nicotiana Falso Nomine Medicaea Appellata 34
Desiderium Lutetiae 22

E Graeco Simonidis (De luce cassis ...) 62
E Graeco Simonidis (Ut arma fugias ...) 20

Index of Poem Titles

Elegy for John Calvin 71
Epithalamium for Francis of Valois and Mary Stuart, Monarchs of France and Scotland 39

For Roger Ascham, Englishman 63
Franciscanus (extract) 2
Francisci Valesi et Mariae Stuartae, Regum Franciae et Scotiae, Epithalamium 38
From the Greek of Simonides (A man can flee ...) 21
From the Greek of Simonides (For just one day ...) 63

Go, Mass is Over 79

Horse Hymn 33
Hymnus Matutinus ad Christum 76

Imago ad Peregre Venientes Religionis Ergo 80
In Eandem Romam 78
In Iulium II Pontificem 78
In Polyonymum 14
In Syllam 64
In Zoilum 16
Inscription for the Tomb of the Portuguese Humanist André de Gouvea 7
Ioannis Calvini Epicedium 70
Ite, Missa Est 78

Jacobo IV. Regi Scotorum 36
Jacobo Sylvio 32

Laurentius Valla 64
Longing for Paris 23
Lorenzo Valla, Humanist 65

Madeleine of Valois, Queen of Scots, Dead at Sixteen 57
Magdalanae Valesiae Reginae Scotorum, XVI Aetatis Anno Exstinctae 56
Mair Leonora 21
Maria Regina Scotiae Puella 36
Morning Hymn to Christ 77
Mutuus Amor 56

Oan Paip J 2 79
On James Wood 33
On the Planet 67

Rogero Aschamo Anglo 62

The Bond of Love 57
The Exorcist 3
The Image to the Pilgrims 81
The Pope of Rome Again 79
The Twenty-third Psalm Paraphrased during Imprisonment at the
    Hands of the Inquisition in Portugal 29
The Young Girl Mary, Queen of Scots 37
To a Bawd called Peiris 19
To Henry Darnley, King of Scots 63
To James IV, King of Scots 37
To Lord Walter Haddon, Petition Master of the Most Serene Queen
    of England 59
To the Noblest Mary, Queen of Scots, with a Book of Psalms 55
To the Opposite of Anon 15
To Theodore Beza 75

XXIII 28

Arthur Johnston

Ad Iamisonum Pictorem, de Anna Cambella, Heroina 132
*Ad Illustrem Comitem Gordonium, Marchionis Huntlaei Filium, Natu
    Maximum* 112
Ad Robertum Baronium (extract) 126
Andreapolis 92

Balagaunius 113
Birthplace 149
Bishop Eudoxus' Doocot 111
Brechin 99
Brechinum 98

De Aberdonia Urbe 100
De Anatomica Sectione, a Iulio Casserio Placentino Patavii Exhibita 106

INDEX OF POEM TITLES

De Balagaunio Eiusdem Equo 112
De Columbario Eudoxi Praesulis 110
De Comite Hollandio 108
De Eiusdem Lapsu ex Equo 114
De Gulielmo Drummondo 142
De Gulielmo Gordonio Rothimaeo, et Georgio Gordonio Caesis 116
De Horto Suo 142
De Hylo Concionatore 144
De Iohanne Gordonio, Vicecomite de Melgein, et Iohanne Gordonio de Rothimay in Arce Frendriaca Combustis 118
De Loco Suo Natali 148
De Reginae Choreis 106
Dundee 95

Edinburgh 87
Edinburgum 86
Elgin 103
Elginum 102
Episcopi Scoti (extract) 104

Four Muses' Sentences 85

Glasgow 89
Glasgua 88

In Obitum Gulielmi Forbesii Cragivarrii 136
In Obitum Iohannae Ionstonae 138
In Obitum M. Davidis Balantini de Kinnochar, Ecclesiastae 130
Inneruria 146
Insignia Equestria Divi Georgii 110
Insignia of the Knights of Saint George 111
Inverurie 147

Mons Rosarum 96
Montrose 97
Musarum Elogia (extract) 84
My Book Garden 143

Nobiles Scoti (extract) 104

Obituary for William Forbes of Craigievar 137
On an Anatomical Dissection Exhibited at Padua by Julius Casserius
   of Placentia 107
On the City of Aberdeen 101
On the Death of Joanna Johnston 139
On the Death of the Reverend David Ballantyne of Kilconquhar 131
On the Earl of Holland 109
On the Fall of the Earl Gordon from his Horse 115
On the Popular Haranguer 'Hylus' Wood 145
On the Queen's Dances 107
On William Drummond 143
On William Gordon of Rothiemay and George Gordon, Killed in
   Action 117

Saltatrix 144
Scots Lords, Scots Bishops 105
St Andrews 93
Sterlinum 90
Stirling 91

Taodunum 94
The Atrocity at Frendrocht 119
The Dancing Art 145
The Tomb of the Noblest Heroine Anne Campbell, Marchioness of
   Huntly 135
To Jamesone the Artist, About the Splendid Lady Anne Campbell 133
To Robert Baron 127
To the Illustrious Earl Gordon, Eldest Son of the Marquis of Huntly 113
Tumulus Nobilissimae Heroinae, Annae Cambellae, Marchionissae de Huntley 134